CALLED TO SUFFER

CHOSEN FOR GREATNESS

By

Cynthia Gibson-Dyse

Called to Suffer, Chosen for Greatness
© 2022 by Cynthia Gibson-Dyse

ISBN-13: 978-1-947288-69-0

All rights reserved solely by the author. Except where designated, the author certifies that all contents are original and do not infringe upon the legal rights of any other person. No part of this book may be reproduced in any form without permission in writing from the publisher, except in the case of brief quotations embodied in critical articles or reviews.

All Scriptures are taken from the King James Version. Scripture quotations marked **NLT** are taken from the Holy Bible, New Living Translation, copyright ©1996, 2004, 2015 by Tyndale House Foundation. Used by permission of Tyndale House Publishers, Carol Stream, Illinois 60188. All rights reserved. Scripture quotations marked **MSG** are taken from The Message, copyright © 1993, 2002, 2018 by Eugene H. Peterson. Used by permission of NavPress. All rights reserved. Represented by Tyndale House Publishers. Scripture quotations marked **AMP** are taken from the Amplified Bible, Copyright © 1954, 1958, 1962, 1964, 1965, 1987 by The Lockman Foundation. Used by permission. Printed in the United States of America. Complete Scripture quotations marked **CJB** are taken from the Complete Jewish Bible by David H. Stern. Copyright © 1998. All rights reserved. Used by permission of Messianic Jewish Publishers, 6120 Day Long Lane, Clarksville, MD 21029. www.messianicjewish.net. Scripture quotations marked **NASB** are taken from the New American Standard Bible®, Copyright © 1960, 1971, 1977, 1995, 2020 by The Lockman Foundation. Used by permission. All rights reserved. www.lockman.org." Scripture quotations marked **GNT** are from the Good News Translation in Today's English Version Second Edition Copyright © 1992 by American Bible Society. Used by Permission. Scripture quotations marked **CEV** are from the Contemporary English Version Copyright © 1991, 1992, 1995 by American Bible Society. Used by Permission. Scripture quotations marked **NIV** are taken from the New International Version® NIV® Copyright © 1973, 1978, 1984, 2011 by Biblica, Inc. Used with permission. All rights reserved worldwide. Scripture quotations marked **TPT** are from The Passion Translation®. Copyright © 2017, 2018, 2020 by Passion & Fire Ministries, Inc. Used by permission. All rights reserved. ThePassionTranslation.com. Scriptures marked **CEB** are taken from the Common English Bible®, **CEB**® Copyright © 2010, 2011 by Common English Bible.™ Used by permission. All rights reserved worldwide.

Printed in the United States of America

10 9 8 7 6 5 4 3 2 1

Cover design by: Legacy Designs, Inc.

Back cover photo by: Kenneth Smith

Published by: Life To Legacy, LLC
P.O. Box 1239
Matteson, IL 60443
www.Life2Legacy.com

Table of Contents

Introduction		5
	Part 1, Suffering Is Inevitable	
1.	Introduction to Suffering, A Great Cloud of Witnesses	9
2.	Why?	23
3.	Purpose In Suffering	30
4.	Suffering from our own Foolish Decisions	44
5.	God as the Source of Suffering	48
6.	God the Ultimate Power	62
7.	Yeah, but I'm Angry	74
8.	Hope Deferred	101
9.	Though	122
	Part 2 Comfort, Peace, and Inspiration: Be of Good Cheer	133
10.	The Promise	136
11.	Called to Greatness	141
12.	Fully Persuaded	144
13.	He Redeems and Restores	147
14.	Singing Through Your Pain	149
15.	Little Strength	153
16.	When the Pain Won't Let Up	158
17.	God Prepares us to Suffer	161
18.	When	164
19.	Abundant Life	166
20.	The God of the Valley	172
21.	The Compassionate Savior	174
22.	Almost	179

Table of Contents

23.	What Does it Look Like to be Blessed	181
24.	Chosen for Greatness	187
25.	When You Suffer from False Accusations	191
26.	Suffering from Sexual Assault	194
27.	Suffering from Mental Illness	198
28.	Triumph in Suffering	203
29.	The Progression of Trouble	207
30.	Low Estate	213
31.	Nevertheless	216
	Epilog	220

Introduction

*Man that is born of a woman is of few days,
and full of trouble.*
Job 14:1

Jesus loves me this I know, for the bible tells me so…, is the opening phrase from a beloved hymn we use to teach our children that Jesus truly loves us. How do we know? The bible tells us so. But there is another truth in the Bible. One that few people like to talk about, and yet it is just as prevalent as his love for us. The truth of pain, trouble, and suffering. The Bible says we will suffer. Yet, when it happens, why do we get so discombobulated? Why is suffering so hard to accept?

It is a fact that life can be full of pain. If you are reading this book, it's probably because you have suffered, you are suffering, or you know someone close to you is suffering. And you want answers. You want to know why is this happening? Why do bad things happen? And why do bad things happen to good people? And why do bad things happen to me? I serve God. I pray. I read my Bible. I obey his word. It seems as if none of that even matters. Why is it that when I need him the most he seems so far away? Every heart seems to ask these questions in times of deep despair and suffering. My heart has asked these questions and more, during some of the darkest times of my life. I truly did not understand why, if God is good, then why am I hurting like this? This situation reminds me of Rebekah when she was pregnant with Jacob and Esau:

> But the children struggled together within her [kicking and shoving one another]; and she said, "If it is so [that the Lord has heard our prayer], why then am I this way?"

> So she went to inquire of the Lord [praying for an answer] Gen. 25:22, AMPC

Rebekah had suffered the shame of being barren for 20 years before she became pregnant with her twin sons. When they began to struggle in her womb, she became distraught. She went from suffering emotionally to suffering physically. The *Complete Jewish Bible* renders Genesis 25:22, like this: "The children fought with each other inside her so much that she said, "If it's going to be like this, why go on living?" What happens when you finally obtain what you have been longing for, and it causes you so much pain that you want to die? Have you ever suffered for so long and then received relief, but that relief ended up causing more pain? When that happens, your response could be like Rebekah's "Why go on living?"

In this book, we examine these questions and more as we navigate through some of the biblical accounts that deal with suffering. You may find yourself surprised at all the suffering that occurred in the Bible. You may also find comfort in the fact that you are not alone in suffering. No one has all the answers to the questions that plague us when we are in the throes of suffering, except God. May his anointing help you find peace and comfort in the pages of this book, and in some of the passages from the Bible that have inspired me.

The first part of this book attempts to provide some explanations for suffering and information about suffering that we generally overlook while reading the Bible. In the second part, I try to offer some comfort, encouragement, and inspiration to help you, the reader, cope with whatever stressors or pain you may be facing. Each chapter in this section can stand on its own. I offer snippets of comfort, encouragements, and information that I have learned through suffering that have helped me immensely. You can read it consecutively, or if you are in the throes of suffering, you can skip to the chapter that you feel will bring you the most comfort at the time, and then return later to read the rest. Finally, you will notice I have added some chapters with original poems by the author. These poems were written during my own times of great suffering. The Lord brought me comfort by giving me words that epitomized my pain and surrounded me in grace.

As this book was in production, I have sent sections of it to people in my life who were hurting and needed answers and immediate comfort. Their response was that those words were a great source of comfort to them during their time of suffering. I hope the words I have written will bless you as it has blessed others.

Part I
Suffering is Inevitable

Chapter One
Introduction to Suffering
A Great Cloud of Witnesses

When you think of suffering in the Bible, does your mind immediately go to Job? Job did suffer terribly, and I will not minimize his suffering, but I would like to introduce you to the "great cloud of witnesses" Job had around him, who also surround us as we suffer in this century, in this lifetime.

Suffering entered this world in the beginning when mankind was expelled from the Garden. Although the Bible only lends a few verses to the incident, don't let this fool you into believing that Adam and Eve did not suffer for their great lapse in judgment. But God, in his great mercy prepared them for the new life outside the Garden and the things they would suffer. "Unto Adam also and to his wife did the Lord God make coats of skins, and clothed them" (Genesis 3:2). They went from wearing nothing because the temperature was perfect in the Garden where they had no struggles or fears, to wearing leather. God was preparing them for the struggle. The thorns and the thistles, the different weather conditions, the toil of life outside the Garden, was quite a transition from paradise in the Garden. God is so compassionate that even in our sin and disobedience he will cover us and prepare us for the consequences we are about to face. He loves us dearly and wants us to succeed. Nevertheless, they still had to suffer the consequences of their disobedience to the word of God.

Can you imagine the splendor of living in a lush garden, the temperature so comfortable you did not even need clothes? Food at your fingertips, and no shame, or fear, or lack? You walk and talk face-to-face daily with God, "THE GOD" that created this amazing paradise. No cooking, no cleaning, no bills, just waking up every day enjoying life. And then, you make one little mistake and that's it! Now you have no home and no ease. Suddenly, you have to struggle to grow your own food, and harvest it. As a result, you start living in shame, fear, want, and every imaginable (and unimaginable) negative condition that transforms your new existence. And the guilt. The guilt of knowing that every time pain is experienced in this world, you were the cause of it. Then one of your sons murders your other son and takes off.

Mary, the mother of Jesus is another person that comes to my mind when I think of suffering. Oh, we glorify her now, posthumously, but have you ever stopped to think about what her life must have been like after people discovered she was pregnant before being married? Back in those days, under the Mosaic law, this was considered a crime, a capital offense. Imagine the shame of walking about in the community seeing the knowing looks, the whispers behind hands, the accusing glances. Think about the fear of the shame of having to tell your family and your new fiancé that you are having a baby that is not his? Then actually experiencing the shame you feared. Think about the trepidation that coursed through her at the thought of the shame she would feel as they looked at her in disgust, disappointment, and maybe even hatred. Then actually feeling that shame when her worries were realized. Imagine the pain of living your truth alone because no one believed you when you told them "This is God's baby". Then, as you approach your delivery date, dealing with the birth pangs under adverse conditions, the agony of walking, or worse yet, riding a donkey to Bethlehem. Having your first baby with no doctor, no mother, in a fowl smelling manger, and substandard conditions to give birth. All of this while still dealing with shame and disgrace that has followed you to your new home. Now let's consider the aftermath when a jealous king gets word that the king of the Jews has been born. King Herod sought to wipe out Jesus by killing all the other babies in the land two-years and under. Consider the survivors guilt Mary experienced after the slaughter of all those innocent babies by the one seeking to kill hers. Watching at the foot of the cross as your son is mercilessly crucified on a lonely hill outside the gates of the city at a place called Calvary.

What about Jeremiah? He did everything right. He was God's prophet. Called at a young age. Chosen by God. Yet he suffered atrociously. We love to quote Jeremiah today, yet he was often ignored and even ridiculed by the people to whom he prophesied. He was persecuted and maligned. He suffered physically and emotionally as he ministered faithfully to God's people. He watched in horror as the nation he loved slid into apostasy, yet he was faithful to his calling and continued to minister to God's people throughout his lifetime.

The prophet Hosea is another powerful example. God actually had him marry a known prostitute who would be unfaithful and have children while committing adultery. Naomi: suffering the loss of both her children and her husband while she was living in a foreign land considered herself to be cursed. Life was treacherous for women back then without a man to cover them and with no posterity to carry on the family line. Joseph the son of Jacob, who was jealously hated, tossed aside and sold into slavery by his own brothers. Finally, King David suffered much because he lived within a family system that was hostile to him, then being pursued by a jealous king trying to snuff out his life.

The stories are too numerous to go on naming individuals in the Bible who experienced suffering. It would take volumes to tell of the agony, anguish, and pain written within the Scriptures. As we read the stories of the suffering of God's people in the pages of our Bible and watch how they remained faithful and turned to their God in times of great suffering, we can come away with a faith that will stand the test of time just as they did.

Why Evil Prevails

> And God said, Let us make man in our image, after our likeness: and let them have dominion over the fish of the sea, and over the fowl of the air, and over the cattle, and over all the earth, and over every creeping thing that creepeth upon the earth.
> Genesis 1:26

> The LORD God made all sorts of trees grow up from the ground—trees that were beautiful and that produced delicious fruit. In the middle of the garden he placed the tree of life and the tree of the knowledge of good and evil. Genesis 2:9, NLT

You will find plenty of treachery and sabotage in the Bible because there has been treachery and sabotage in the earth since man was given free-will. It was their decision to choose evil over good and cause pain to others, and the bible records it. Nevertheless, God's plans are not thwarted by man's choice of evil. Neither is God ever surprised by the evil happening in our world but is always able to redeem it so that it works for our good if we turn to him and put our trust in him and his power. In the beginning God gave dominion and free-will to man. Good and evil were always present, but mankind had no knowledge of it. Every day was the same. Every day they were with God in the Garden. But, they didn't realize they were in the presence of Love incarnate. They didn't know what they felt in his presence was great joy, or peace, or goodness, because there was no knowledge of these emotions. To them every day was just meh. Just another day in the Garden. Because without the knowledge of good and evil there is no joy, or happiness, or ecstasy, there is only "meh". It was God's plan for mankind to only experience good and live in relationship with him always. However, he did want to be chosen. He wanted man to have a choice about whether or not he would live in relationship with him (God). Because love isn't love unless it's a choice. If it isn't given freely, it's not love. So, God gifted mankind with free-will. Today we still have that same free-will. He lets us choose to believe in him or not. Yes us. Mere little stupid mortals get to choose if we are going to believe in the Being that created us. Isn't that wild? But that's just like God. He's so wild, and funny, and loving, and kind. And he really desires a relationship with his creation. Us.

God gave mankind free-will to choose between good and evil. Whether to walk with God or do it on our own. Choice. When there is no choice there is no freedom, and no appreciation for the good we experience because there is no difference. When man used his free-will to eat of the tree that God had commanded him not to, he chose evil over good and relinquished his dominion to the forces of evil. All he had left was free-will. When others choose to use their free-will to choose evil it affects everyone. As a result, good people often suffer because of another's choice. Our free-will does not affect only us, because we are all connected. But when Jesus died on the cross, he took back our dominion. Now, when we turn to him, we can get our dominion back. He wants us to have dominion again. And he wants to take all our pain, disappointments, fear, anger, rejection, abandonment, and replace them with peace—pure, unadulterated peace. He wants to hold you and whisper "I'll never leave you," until your fears go away. But he can't unless you choose to believe that he exists and that he wants to do that for you.

God has the power to make us do everything that he wants us to do. But to do that he would have to remove free-will from the equation. Serial killers and all manner of evil people would have to act right, but we wouldn't have any choice in our lives either. Yes, God created good and evil for our choice. But he also extremely loved us that he gave his only begotten Son that whoever chose to believe on him would not have to perish but would live forever with him (John 3:16). The problem is that some of the "whoevers" in this world choose evil, and their decision to choose evil affects everyone else's choice. Life was never meant to be so painful. But God has a plan that he created from the foundation of the earth, because he knows the end from the beginning. And he knew how man would choose. He created a plan to redeem us, and when it's all over, let us live with him in all the peace, joy, and beauty of his original plan. He showed the Apostle John a vision of this beautiful place, and John wrote about it in the book of Revelation.

> So he took me in the Spirit to a great, high mountain, and he showed me the holy city, Jerusalem, descending out of heaven from God. It shone with the glory of God and sparkled like a precious stone-like jasper as clear as crystal.
>
> And the city has no need of sun or moon, for the glory of God illuminates the city, and the Lamb is its light. The nations will walk in its light, and the kings of the world will enter the city in all their glory. Its gates will never be closed at the end of day because there is no night there.
>
> Nothing evil will be allowed to enter, nor anyone who practices shameful idolatry and dishonesty-but only those whose names are written in the Lamb's Book of Life. Rev. 21:10-11, 23-25, 27, NLT

This is that "hope of an expected end" the prophet Jeremiah talks about. As Paul said in his first letter to the Corinthians, "if the only thing I had to hope in was this life and what happens to me during this time on earth, I would be the most miserable person there ever was" (1 Cor. 15:19 I paraphrased the Apostle Paul). But because I have a God to believe in, something outside myself, that's bigger than me or anything that can happen to me I'm okay. As a matter of fact, I am more than okay. Sometimes, I even rejoice when things look so bad. When my circumstances don't line up with what a "good life" should look like, I can have joy, and peace, and comfort in the knowledge that there is a God. I am truly assured that he truly loves me and is for me. Therefore, hope rises up within me. I can get through another day. I can walk by faith because I know I don't have to do this in my own power. When I am suffering, and in agony and fear begins to set in, I know I am not alone, and I know I don't have to deal with the pain in my own strength. None of us can deal with our inner most pain like God. We can't do this by ourselves. And the good news is, we don't have to. That's what the word gospel means, *good news*. All we have to do is believe. You don't have to understand to believe. As a matter of fact, faith is believing when you don't understand. If you understood God, he wouldn't be a god.

Did you know that you already have faith? You believe in President Lincoln even though you have never seen him, (by the way there are still scandals coming out on him so....). You believe that a chair you've never sat in will hold you up when you go to sit in it. You believe when you get in your car and drive, that you will get to your destination and back even though many people die in car accidents every day. You fly in airplanes, ride boats, fall in love, get married. All these actions take faith. It's there!

Trusting and faith are an act of will. God gave us free-will to choose. Though fear can physically invade our senses, we can still choose to trust. We can enact our will and choose not to fear anything humans can do to us. Jesus said to his disciples: "Let not your heart be troubled: ye believe in God, believe also in me" (John 14:1) and "Let not your heart be troubled, neither let it be afraid" (John 14:27b). These scriptures imply that we are able to control our hearts. To "let" something happen or not means you have control over it. It means that we are in control of our fear and not the other way around. This concept can be so hard to grasp when you're in the midst of a fear inducing situation. But the Bible also says, "let God be true; but every man a liar" (Romans 3:4). If God says we can, then we can. So even when my body is afraid, I can engage my mind and my mouth to be bold and courageous. I can speak faith into my heart. I can choose to only say what God says about me and about my situation. I can choose to believe. I can choose faith, the evidence of things not seen. So, when False Evidence Appears Real (F.E.A.R.), faith is the evidence I should choose to believe. That's why the Bible says we walk by faith and not by sight. Faith is substance, something we can hold onto. We do not need any other substance.

"Bless (In the Hebrew means, *kneel down before*) the LORD, O my soul, And all that is within me, bless His holy name" (Psalm 103:1,

NASB). Sometimes you have to force your body and everything within you to bow before his majesty. Because in our humanity we tend to forget all the benefits we have in serving the one true and living God when we are suffering. Consistently in the Psalms, David remembered God's character and the benefits of having a god who was bigger than anything that could happen to him during times of great suffering. David went back to the word of God to find comfort and direction during painful times.

In the 103rd Psalm, David commands everything inside of him to kneel before God. His soul, which is the mind, will, and emotions; and anything else within. So, whether it is depression—it has to bow. If it is anxiety—it has to bow. Low self-esteem—bow down! Pride-get on your knees! Anger, bitterness, hatred—take a knee! We can command everything in our inward self to bow down before the name of Jesus and be subject to the Lord's majesty. If we run to him, we can find safety in his name and be raised high above any danger that would come to harm us.

"The name of ADONAI is a strong tower; a righteous person runs to it and is raised high [above danger]" (Proverbs 18:10, CJB). The name of Jesus is above every name. Nothing can stand before it. As God's children we have the privilege of declaring the name of Jesus over our problems and watching from the high place as he deals with the danger that was threatening us. The *King James Version* of this verse says this: "The name of the LORD is a strong tower: the righteous runneth into it and is safe." The word "safe" can be translated as *set aloft* as in, out of the reach of harm or danger or turmoil. A strong tower is an inaccessible place. The righteous have access, but the wicked cannot. To have access to an inaccessible place you either have to have a good relationship with someone in charge or be that person. David had a good relationship with the one in charge.

LONGSUFFERING

Endure

By Cynthia Gibson-Dyse

Endure when you are lonely.
Endure when you are sad.
Endure when things seem hopeless.
Endure when things seem bad.
Endure when you are getting weak
And can't hold on much longer;
Endurance is the very thing
That makes the weakling stronger.
Endure when the enemy surrounds you
And you have nowhere to hide.
Stand your ground, don't give up
For God is on your side.
Hold to God's unchanging hand
On Him you can depend.
For the prize isn't given to those who start
But to those who endure to the end.

HOW LONG?

By Cynthia Gibson-Dyse

How long Lord, how long?

My soul crieth to Thee.

Be still child, be still.

Was your answer to me.

Why me Lord, why me?

My heart cried out in pain.

Trust me child, trust me.

Was all that he would say.

The earth is the fullness of the Lord

And all that lieth within.

My help cometh from the Lord.

And I will wait on him.

How long must I struggle with anguish in my soul, with sorrow in my heart every day? How long will my enemy have the upper hand? Turn and answer me, O Lord my God! Restore the sparkle to my eyes, or I will die. Don't let my enemies gloat, saying, "We have defeated him!" Don't let them rejoice at my downfall. (rejoice not over me oh my enemies Micah 7:8) But I trust in your unfailing love. I will rejoice because you have rescued me. Psalms 13:2-5, NLT

The prophet Habakkuk asked these same questions. "How long?" How long will you allow good people to suffer with the bad? How long will you allow wicked people to prosper? How long will injustice prevail? Don't you see the injustice? Can't you hear our cries?" I have felt that way, often. I have asked God those same questions. I wrote the poem "How Long" one day as I pondered this quandary. David's Psalm addressed it. Habakkuk cried it. Job probably thought it as he scraped his festering sores. Jeremiah may have yelled it from the empty cistern. Maybe Mary, the mother of Jesus thought it as she walked the streets of her town, falsely accused, looked down on, sneered at, talked about, and yet, she was innocent. She had done no wrong. Night after night, as Hosea tossed in his bed, wondering where his wayward wife was. He searched the streets for her only to find her in the arms of an illicit lover. As she brought home baby after baby that he knew was not his, these questions must have tumbled over and over in his mind. And if you are reading this book, you may have asked these questions too.

When it seems like God is just sitting idly by, ignoring our cause, yes, we will ask the questions. However, after the questions have been asked and even though they have not been answered, the second thing we must do is turn to the word of God, and seek to know his character. When we know God's character, nothing can separate us from his love. He said, "be still and know that I Am God" (Psalm 46:10). The word "know" in this scripture is the Hebrew *yada* which means *to know intimately*. If you know God intimately then you must know he is a God that loves justice.

Third, be still. Sit with him and invite him to sit with you. God wants to be intimate with us. "He is nigh to those of a broken heart…" (Psalm 34:18). He created us for intimate relationship. He wants to touch us. Man is the only part of creation God touched when he created him. Everything else was spoken into being. But from the beginning God touched our lives. And the scripture declares God is the same yesterday, today, and forever (See Hebrews 13:8). His desire to be with us has not changed.

Fourth, remember who "I Am" is. "I Am" is everything you need him to be. He is present. He's not "I will be." "Am" denotes the present tense, he always "is." His character does not change. You can count on that. He is the unfailing God.

Fifth, if you know who he is, you need to know whose you are. You need to know that you belong to him. If you have accepted him as your Savior, live like he is. What is a Savior? Someone who will save you from whatever you need saving from. Someone who will keep you safe. I can trust a savior. If I belong to a God who is a savior, I don't have to worry about evil. I am safe. I can trust in a savior. I can lean heavily on a savior.

The perfect answer to injustice is to know who your God is, and know his power and love for you. The three Hebrew boys (Shadrach, Meshach, and Abednego) knew who their God was and refused to worship any other, even under the threat of death and great suffering. David knew who his God was and wrote many Psalms to acknowledge the true and living God. Habakkuk knew who his God was and sat upon his watch to wait on him. Job knew who his God was and was blessed all the more for it. Jeremiah knew who his God was, and stated, "The Lord is my portion, saith my soul, therefore will I hope in Him" (Lamentations 3:24). Mary, the mother of Jesus, knew who her God was and said, "My soul doth magnify the Lord" (Luke 1:46). Hosea knew who his God was and warned: *"My people are destroyed for lack of knowledge"* (Hosea 4:6). And I know who my God is, and I am writing this book in hopes that it will help you know him too.

Called To Suffer

SOMETIMES WE CRY
By Cynthia Gibson-Dyse

Sometimes we cry, sometimes we ask why?

Sometimes we just sit and stare.

Sometimes we groan, there are times we even moan because we feel life's so unfair.

Sometimes we weep. Sometimes we lose sleep.

Sometimes we'd like to run away.

Sometimes we sigh,

Sometimes we'd like to die because we can't make it through another day.

Sometimes we want to mope. Sometimes we give up hope. Sometimes we even fall.

Sometimes we're full of gloom when no one's in the room and there's no one we can call.

But take comfort my friend all this will end when Jesus calls his church away.

There'll be no more night. We'll be walking in the light. It will be one happy day!

There'll be no reason to cry, no reason to ask why; no time to sit and stare.

There'll be no reason to moan, we'll never even groan, because Jesus will be there.

There'll be no cause to weep, we'll have no need of sleep, and no need to run away.

There'll be no need to sigh, and we'll never ever die; Just one happy joy filled day!

We won't want to mope. There'll be no need of hope, and we'll surely never fall.

No days filled with gloom. No more empty room. There'll be no pain at all!

Just take comfort my friend, a new life will begin when we enter that pearly gate.

Lift your head to the sky, your redemption draweth nigh.

Heaven, I can hardly wait!

Chapter Two

Why?

What do the words *por que* (Spanish), and *pourquoi* (French) have in common? They both mean *why*. The first question that often arises when we suffer is why? Why is this happening to me? As a clinical social worker, and a Christian, I have heard this question often when it comes to suffering. It doesn't matter what language you say it in, it's still a cry from a confused heart that wants to know "what is the meaning of this?" This question opens the floodgates of the doubts just waiting to press in on us. Pressing out the little mustard seed of faith we had left. Is God for me? If God is for me, how could he let this happen to me? If he is all powerful and loves me, then why doesn't he do something to change this, stop this, fix this...? This opens the door to confusion, disappointment, anxiety depression, and other evil works.

Jeremiah was so confused at being punished. He had done everything right. He hadn't turned away from God as the people had. Yet he was lumped right in with them. In Jeremiah 15:18, the prophet cried out to God: "Why is my pain perpetual, and my wound incurable, which refuseth to be healed? wilt thou be altogether unto me as a liar, and as waters that fail?" Has that ever happened to you? Have you ever suffered for something you didn't even do? You didn't have any part in and yet you were lumped in with everyone else who was culpable, and you asked why? Did you ever feel like even God was against you unrighteously? Did you ask Why?

Rebekah was perplexed when she became pregnant with twins and was suffering due to this pregnancy. Habakkuk was baffled at all the injustice and suffering God's people were dealing with in captivity.

Gideon was confused and a little disappointed in God when the angel came to inform him that God was with his people and he wanted to use Gideon to rescue his people from the Midianites. *"Sir, Gideon replied, if the Lord is with us, why has all this happened to us? And where are all the miracles our ancestors told us about? Didn't they say, 'The Lord brought us up out of Egypt'? But now the Lord has abandoned us and handed us over to the Midianites." (Judges 6:13, NLT).* Gideon's answer to the Angel was a little "salty". When you don't understand the reasons behind your pain, bitterness can lurk in the dark corners of your heart and make it very difficult for you to see God's goodness. Jeremiah almost called God a liar. Gideon called him out on his rescue flop.

As humans we have the ability to reason, but when it comes to suffering this ability often seems to fail us. I have grappled with confusion many times as I navigated the many tear-filled nights that suffering brought to my life. As a matter of fact, helping others (and myself) wrestle with this question was the impetus for this book. I have learned to turn to the pages of the bible (or my bible apps) and to my relationship with God to help make sense of this universal struggle.

The Bible is full of stories of suffering. The story of Lazarus and his sisters is a story about mental, physical, and emotional suffering. In the book of St John chapter 11, it tells us that a certain man was sick. And it gives us his name (Lazarus) and the name of his two sisters, Mary and Martha, and it says that Jesus loved this family, and they loved him. But the dilemma comes when Lazarus becomes very sick and dies. And even though Mary and Martha sent for Jesus while Lazarus was still alive (because they had witnessed Jesus perform many miracles of healing on many strangers and sinners) they had hope that their friend Jesus was going to come and heal their brother, whom he loved. But even though Jesus was close enough to come in time to perform a healing miracle for his friends he did not come when he got word of the need. The bible says: *"When he had heard therefore that he was sick, he abode two days still in the same place where he was" (11:6).* Ouch! What a blow to our relationship!

We often think, "if only God would come and fix this or save us from that." Just like Mary and Martha, we wish God would come when we want him, need him. But he doesn't come, and we suffer. Why? Why does God allow it? Sometimes when we suffer, it just has to be. Sometimes it has to be for God to get glory. Sometimes he's getting glory over his enemies, and sometimes he's getting glory over ours. What really glorifies God? Does it glorify him more for us to have riches and wealth and health in this world? Or does he get more glory if we don't receive riches or relief from our suffering but still live a life of peace, contentment and worship?

Jesus informed his disciples concerning Lazarus' sickness that: "…This sickness is not unto death, but for the glory of God, that the Son of God might be glorified thereby" (John 11:4). What do you mean it's not unto death? Two days later Jesus told his disciples that Lazarus had died. Have you ever been confused by conflicting information? Okay, I know God loves me, the Bible says it and I believe it. But this thing I'm going through is hard, painful, and it's tough. My reality is not measuring up to my expectations. When I became a Christian, I expected God to help me. I expected my life to get easier. But sometimes I cry, "What's really going on here?"

When we suffer, especially when it seems unfair, we can fall into an attitude of despair and self-pity. This attitude opens us to doubt about God's faithfulness, goodness, and love for us. This is so offensive to God. How do you feel when you've only done good to people and they misjudge you and accuse you of unrighteousness or abuse? Sitting between the tension of God's love for us and our suffering we discover his sovereignty. As Job asked "Mrs. Job", *"shall we receive good at the hand of God and not receive evil?"* (Job 2:10). In times of suffering, it is important to remember that God is sovereign. He can do whatever he pleases, whenever he pleases. He can allow good, or he can allow evil, and we need to get with his program. He doesn't have to fit into ours. But please know that if he allows it his purpose is greater than our pain.

God knew the anguish Hannah would go through by not being able to conceive a child. Yet it was God that closed Hannah's womb. As a result of this she experienced humiliation in her own home, while in her community she also had to deal with the stigma of not being able to have a child. Add to this the sadness and longing for a child just because she was a Jewish woman who longed to be included in God's promise to Eve. God is acutely aware of all the suffering in the world. The genocides, slavery, the Holocaust, human trafficking. Why does he allow it?

Some seem to think that God's sovereignty means we can't ask him questions, like "why is this happening to me?" Or "what's going on?" But this isn't so. While it is okay to ask God questions, it's not okay to *question* him. There's a difference. People who asked God questions received answers. People who questioned God received rebuke and consequences for lack of faith. Because without faith it is impossible to please God. As a matter of fact, even Jesus asked God questions. We see this in Mark 15:34, "And at the ninth hour Jesus cried with a loud voice, saying, Eloi, Eloi, lama sabachthani! Which is, being interpreted, My God, my God, why hast thou forsaken me?" Even Jesus, the son of God felt like God had forsaken him and had to ask why. But we see here that in his suffering he turned to God and not away. Jesus is our example. We should always turn to God in suffering. It's okay to ask him the hard questions. Why Lord? Why? Where are you, Lord? When Lord? When will you rescue me?

God wants us to share our suffering with him. Through prayer we can share our feelings with God. This allows him to take part in our good times and our suffering. This is the mark of a good relationship. He created us for relationship, and what kind of relationship is it if you can't ask questions? Questions are a part of communication, and good communication builds relationships. God just doesn't want you to argue with him or question his motives. Actually, the right response when we suffer, even if we think it's undeserved is to go to the source. It's ok to ask God why. But you must prepare your heart and mind for his answer. God did answer Jeremiah just as he answered Job:

> Therefore, thus says the LORD [to Jeremiah], "If you repent [and give up this mistaken attitude of despair

> and self-pity], then I will restore you [to a state of inner peace] So that you may stand before Me [as My obedient representative]; And if you separate the precious from the worthless [examining yourself and cleansing your heart from unwarranted doubt concerning My faithfulness], You will become My spokesman. Let the people turn to you [and learn to value My values]— But you, you must not turn to them [with regard for their idolatry and wickedness]. And I will make you to this people A fortified wall of bronze; They will fight against you, But they will not prevail over you, For I am with you [always] to save you And protect you," says the LORD."
> Jeremiah 15:19-20, AMP

When we turn to God with a heart full of faith and a worshipful attitude, he may eventually help us understand. Recognizing God's sovereignty is worship. But we may never fully understand the whys of suffering in this life. Paul told the Corinthians: "Now our knowledge is partial and incomplete, and even the gift of prophecy reveals only part of the whole picture" (1 Corinthians 13:9, NLT).

Furthermore, people are asking this question all over the globe. "Why me?" Why do I suffer so? Why do I suffer with depression, anxiety, bipolar disorder, cancer, lupus, chronic pain, emotional pain, and trauma? Why me? And I don't have the answer. But could it be for such a time as this?

> Mordecai sent this reply to Esther: "Don't think for a moment that because you're in the palace you will escape when all other Jews are killed. If you keep quiet at a time like this, deliverance and relief for the Jews will arise from some other place, but you and your relatives will die. Who knows if perhaps you were made queen for just such a time as this?" Esther 4:13-14, NLT

The enemy of our souls will work very hard to destroy someone whose life holds greatness. Moses and Jesus were two of the greatest men who ever walked the earth. The enemy was aware of the time of their birth and attempted to destroy them before their [this] ever made it into this earth realm. The greatness God put inside you at conception is your "this". What is your this? Is it the time you sat by a stranger on a train, a bus, or in an airport, and shared your story? Did you greet a visitor at church and give them a smile even though you were obviously in pain? Will someone someday read about you in a book like we read about Job and say, "if God is able to keep them, he can keep me too?" What is your this? Sometimes our this is just to be an example of God's power to keep us. Sometimes just to show his power to resurrect, as he did with Lazarus. Lazarus was just an ordinary man who loved Jesus, yet his fame went out through the land and to us today, after Jesus resurrected him. He was a witness of God's power just waking up each morning. When he walked into a room, did people recognize him as the man Jesus raised from the dead? Here many Jews became believers due to Lazarus' resurrection. The raising of Lazarus was the final miraculous proof to the Hebrews that Jesus was Messiah. He had raised others from the dead, but they were newly dead. Lazarus was completely dead in the eyes of that culture. His death, and subsequently resurrection was indisputable. What indisputable attribute does your suffering hold? How can God be glorified through you?

You have to ask yourself, "why is the devil so afraid of me?" What greatness is in you that he has to keep after you? Remember Moses and Jesus? The devil tried to destroy them before they reached greatness. The gates of hell shall not prevail against God's Church. You are in his Church and the gates of hell will not prevail. But they will try. You are more than a conqueror. So, if you never get an answer on this side of heaven as to why you are suffering, don't put any more energy into it and just worship the God that is in complete control of the universe and all that he created. In the 46th Psalm he said, "Be still and know that I am God."

God's Tapestry

By: Cynthia Gibson-Dyse

I came to God on my knees in prayer,

and through repentance he met me there.

A wonderful feeling came over me;

it was the beginning of God's tapestry.

As I walked with him, he wove in me

the beautiful threads of his tapestry.

I couldn't see them for he worked in parts;

he used threads of suffering and broken hearts,

I was tired and confused as he wove in and out;

but he's the Master of Weavers so I shook off the doubt.

He can make a great picture of the tears that I cry,

although when I cry them, I often ask why?

I can't see the picture for I'm on the wrong side,

but one day I'll see if his threads I'll abide.

It will be the best artwork you ever did see,

because nothing compares to God's tapestry.

Chapter Three

Purpose In Suffering

For we are God's masterpiece. He has created us anew in Christ Jesus, so we can do the good things he planned for us long ago.
Eph. 2:10, NLT

We are God's masterpiece. He had a plan in mind for our lives before we ever entered the world. God weaves the threads of suffering into the fabric of our lives just as a weaver uses dark threads to create a beautiful tapestry, or a painter uses the contrast of light and dark and various colors to create a masterpiece. God is the creator of creators. He understands the need for contrast and balance in life as well as in all of creation. And suffering, in God's hands, are the dark threads he uses to create the contrast needed to create the beauty that is us. God uses suffering in many ways, but his intentions are always good. But while we are going through the test or trial, we can easily become confused because all we have seen is evil. We become habituated to evil so that when we see good, true goodness, it is hard for us to comprehend it.

Evil perpetuates evil. Violence perpetuates violence. Negativity perpetuates negativity. This is the reason so many people have difficulty believing that God loves them. For instance, if your natural father was absent, or abusive, or mean, or authoritarian, and you never saw any other male figure demonstrate other qualities, then it could be very difficult to see God as a loving, kind, gentle, compassionate father. When you hear the word "father" it doesn't bring up images of going fishing and being nurtured. No, it will bring up images from your childhood of being hurt and abused, and it is so easy to project this hurt onto God. We see this in the 17th chapter of Jeremiah. He felt he was suffering wrongfully and became lost in his feelings of hurt that were being perpetrated upon him by God's people whom God had sent him to prophesy to.

This is the suffering Peter wrote about in 1 Peter 2:20-21

> ... if you endure suffering even when you have done right, God will bless you for it. It was to this that God called you, for Christ himself suffered for you and left you an example, so that you would follow in his steps. GNT

Peter goes so far as to say that we were actually called to suffer like Christ. And we were. But everyone who was called to suffer in the Bible were actually chosen for greatness. And so it is still today. I can name numerous examples of great men and women who have suffered greatly in this century, but before everything was all said and done it was revealed that their suffering only preceded their greatness. King David said in retrospect "it is good for me that I have been afflicted" (Psalm 119:71). *The New Living Translation* says it this way, "My suffering was good for me, for it taught me to pay attention to your decrees."

Sometimes *it is* God's will for us to suffer. Sometimes *we will* look bad, as bad as a plant that has been pruned. If you're afraid to look bad, you'll never do God's will. God will let you look bad. He will prune you until you're naked and you feel there's nothing left. But the ways of the Lord are right. "Who is wise, and he shall understand these things? prudent, and he shall know them? for the ways of the Lord are right, and the just shall walk in them: but the transgressors shall fall therein" (Hosea 14:9). David said: "Thou preparest a table before me in the presence of mine enemies" (Psalm 23:5a). So often we fear the fact that we may have enemies. But enemies are needed for us to have victory. How can God give us victory over our enemies if we don't have any? How can he prepare a table before us in the presence of our enemies if we don't have any haters? How can he get the glory if our life is full of ease and satisfaction?

Sometimes troubles can come so fast and seemingly out of nowhere that it seems as if God is capricious, and we are tempted to blame him and turn away from him. But let me assure you my friend, God is not capricious, but he is purposeful, and good, and every situation we go through is monitored by him. Though he doesn't always cause it, he sits as the refiner of silver and uses the heat of our afflictions to burn off the dross (impurities, worthless matter, things that are in us that shouldn't be) so that he can eventually see himself reflected in us. *"Christ that is in us, the hope of glory" (Colossians 1:27).* But there are other times when even though God doesn't tempt us, he leads us into temptation. As stated in Matthew 4:1, *"Then was Jesus led up of the Spirit into the wilderness to be tempted of the devil.* The first time God spoke to Hosea he said: *"Find a whore and marry her. Make this whore the mother of your children. And here's why: This whole country has become a whorehouse, unfaithful to me, GOD" (Hosea 1:2 MSG).* Although God did not tempt Jesus nor Hosea, he did allow them to be tempted. He even led them there.

Both Mary and Joseph endured great shame giving birth to the savior. Other people, even her own family did not believe she was giving birth to the savior. People assumed she and Joseph had come together before marriage. Yet, God had sent an angel to them to inform them that he had chosen them for this very difficult, pain filled task. And they agreed to it.

Don't be surprised if God leads you into temptation. Jesus knew and warned us to pray that we enter not into temptation, and he even modeled it in the Lord's Prayer: "and lead us not into temptation...." But if God does lead us into temptation, we have assurance that he will lead us out, because David said, "He leads me in paths of righteousness" (Ps. 23:3). God is righteous.

Everything God does is right. We don't have to fear failure or looking bad. God is a god of purpose. He can redeem any situation to meet his purpose. "And we know that God causes everything to work together for the good of those who love God and are called according to his purpose for them" (Romans 8:28, NLT). Have you ever prayed for God to take away your pain? You're in good company. Paul prayed three times for him to take away the thorn in his flesh, and Jesus, God's own son, prayed three times not to have to go to the cross and feel that agony. God is able to take pain away, but *If* he allows it to stay it has a purpose. When you ask why or how long, maybe you're asking the wrong question. Perhaps you should ask what is the purpose in my pain? Has it made me more sensitive to others in the same situation? Has it made me a better parent for my children? Has it made me a better citizen in my community? Of this earth? Pause and think, what can this pain teach me?

Focus energy into figuring out how you can use your pain to help others. Purpose is built-in pain relief. You know what God told Paul? "My grace is sufficient for thee, my strength is made perfect in weakness" (2 Corinthians 12:9). Paul's sufferings were to reveal the grace of God to us. Our struggles are for us to reveal the grace of God to our world. All of our struggles have purpose. Have you surrendered your life totally to Christ? Surrender to Christ is the key to unlock grace. To them that have received him to them gave he power to become the sons of God (John 1:12 my paraphrase). You can depend on God to give you the power to become everything you need to become, if you receive him. Then you will be more than a conqueror. And you will be persuaded that nothing can separate you from his love.

Yes, we suffer. And yes, it is painful. But we have this treasure in earthen vessels, that the excellency of the power may be of God (God purposefully allows us to appear weak so that others looking on will see his glory and his power), and not of us. When others see us going through and not turning away from God but turning to him. Oh, what glory goes to him!

> We are troubled on every side, yet not distressed; we are perplexed, but not in despair; Persecuted, but not forsaken; cast down, but not destroyed; Always bearing about in the body the dying of the Lord Jesus, that the life also of Jesus might be made manifest in our body.
> 2 Cor. 4:7-10

I love this scripture. I have been in this place of trouble, perplexed, cast down. And I am a living witness that I have not been destroyed by it. Instead, I have been strengthened by it. Jesus was made manifest in me when I forgave those who tried to distress me. My body became his when I stood up to troubles and did not break. When those who I thought would love me forever cast me down and aside and I was not destroyed. While others looked at my life and saw Jesus, his purpose in my suffering was fulfilled.

God Uses Suffering to Prove Us

> And the people murmured against Moses, saying, What shall we drink? And he cried unto the Lord; and the Lord shewed him a tree, which when he had cast into the waters, the waters were made sweet: there he made for them a statute and an ordinance, and there he proved them. Exodus 15:24-25

> …I proved thee at the waters of Meribah. Selah.
> Psalm 81:7

What do you do when times get hard? When you are suffering and you don't understand? Do you complain to other people about it? Do you get bitter and angry and throw up your hands and walk away? Do you pray about it, and it seems as if God totally does not get it?

In the 15th chapter of Exodus, after a great victory, a miracle of God parting waters for his people to escape their enemy, they ran into another hard situation. They had a vital need and it seemed as if God was not going to help this time. All he gave them were the tools to get what they needed. As a matter of fact, he didn't actually give them anything, he just showed their leader a tree. And they let their leader have it. They began to murmur and complain.

God was "proving them." A synonym for "proving" is "establishing." God was establishing the fact that he was their God and provider, and they should look to him with expectancy and worship, and he would supply their needs on this journey. Instead, they proved to him that they were bitter, angry, spoiled children with rotten attitudes.

God took care of their need in spite of their attitude, but he was not pleased. You are God's child. He is going to take care of your needs. But your attitude determines how he blesses you. They complained so much until God decided to wait until that whole generation was dead before fulfilling his promise of taking his people into the Promised Land.

When things don't go your way and you get angry with God, you are acting just like the children of Israel. God kept doing mighty wonders for them, but every time things got a little hard for them they turned against him and blamed him. Selah (pause and calmly think about this). Do you really want to be like them? They missed out on so much of his goodness that he had prepared for them. Learn to turn TO God and worship him when trouble comes. You will experience his goodness more and more and your faith will be unshakable.

Why does God test us when he already knows everything about us? So that we will know our own limits. Not so that we will know them and stop there. But so that when we come to our limits, and we go beyond them we will know that it was only God that could have done that in our lives. So that we will know how great God is and how powerful he is. He is "proving" us. Proving brings about worship if we let it, if we open our hearts to an all-powerful God.

> And thou shalt remember all the way which the Lord thy God led thee these forty years in the wilderness, to humble thee, and to prove thee, to know what was in thine heart, whether thou wouldest keep his commandments, or no.   Deuteronomy 8:2

The word *prove* in this instance means to show the Israelites what was in them. God is the only one who knows the human heart. He understands that it is "desperately wicked" and "deceitful," so he searches the heart and tests the mind to let us see what's inside our own heart, because he knows that our lives consist of the results of what is in our hearts (Jeremiah 17:9, 10; Proverbs 23:7).

God already knew their lack of faith, the fear that resided in them. Their propensity to bow down when things got difficult was not hidden from his sight. He wanted them to *yada* (Hebrew for *to know*) this and to get an intimate understanding that he was their God. And he wanted them to know that he was with them and would always take care of them as no other God ever had or ever would or could take care of their people. God had a plan. And he has a plan for your life too. God wants us to seek him, and to know him, and to know what is in our hearts. Not just so we can have the knowledge, but that we can know it and correct it, or bring it to him to correct for us.

He also wanted to teach them that he will show up when he says he will. He gave them daily bread. They had to show up daily to collect it and he showed up daily to provide it. So, you ask the question: "what about the sabbath, he didn't show up on the sabbath?" No, he wanted to teach them that he is sovereign. That he will show up when he says he will, and we don't get to choose his timing. If he says wait, then we should wait. If he says go, then we should go. Just like the lesson of the moving cloud, when God got ready to move in the cloud, they had to pack up and move. If he stayed, they had to stay as long as he did, and wait on him.

Staying and waiting on instructions equals relationship. Good relationships are built on trust. God wants to have a good relationship with his people. He wants us to show up daily and talk to him. He wants us to need him daily. And he wants us to trust him. God's response to our situations is based in his sovereignty and not weakness. He is always for us even when it looks like things or circumstances are against us. The answer often lies in us waiting on him. Peter told the "Elect" church in his first letter to them:

> …These trials will show that your faith is genuine. It is being tested as fire tests and purifies gold—though your faith is far more precious than mere gold. So when your faith remains strong through many trials, it will bring you much praise and glory and honor on the day when Jesus Christ is revealed to the whole world. … Though you do not see him now, you trust him; and you rejoice

> with a glorious, inexpressible joy. The reward for trusting him will be the salvation of your souls.
>
> 1 Peter 1:6-9, NLT

Yes, God uses suffering to prove us, but afterwards, there is a great reward.

God Uses Suffering to Discipline Us

"Know then in your heart that as a man disciplines his son, so the Lord your God disciplines you" (Deuteronomy 8:5, NIV).

The definition of the word "discipline" here is on a spectrum. From speaking words of correction, all the way to beating with a rod. In the Bible we see this whole spectrum manifested in the ways God disciplines his people. He used prophets and serpents and plagues and wars. He spoke from a cloud and sent famines and floods, all to get the attention of the people he loved. God's ultimate goal in discipline is our righteousness.

> No discipline is enjoyable while it is happening—it's painful! But afterward there will be a peaceful harvest of right living for those who are trained in this way.
>
> Hebrews 12:11, NLT

When we are in the throes of suffering it can be hard to believe that God even cares, or indeed loves us. Just like when we were children and were disciplined by our parents and it felt as if they hated us. But as adults we understand that our parents loved us and did the best they could to help us to change the things they knew would end up ultimately causing us pain. (At least those of us who were fortunate enough to have had at least one good caring parent). The Bible tells us not to despise, or reject the chastening or correction from the Lord, but that our attitude should be one of gladness, or joy because if he corrects us, in the end it will bring about righteousness for us (See Proverbs 3:11, 15:32, Job 5:17, Hebrews 12:7-11).

Throughout the Bible, God had to chasten his chosen people. Today, we are his chosen people. He will chasten us and test our hearts if we will allow him so that we can be his own. In reading the Bible you will find many places that God used suffering to discipline his people. From the Garden of Eden to the last chapter of the last book, God demonstrated his sovereignty and love through suffering.

The whole third chapter of Lamentations gives perspective on suffering due to God's wrath.

> "I am the man that hath seen affliction by the rod of his wrath. It is good that a man should both hope and quietly wait for the salvation of the Lord. It is good for a man that he bear the yoke in his youth. He giveth his cheek to him that smiteth him: he is filled full with reproach. Wherefore doth a living man complain, a man for the punishment of his sins?
> Lamentations 3:1, 26-27, 30, 39

It is good to be afflicted by God for sin. God uses punishment to help us remember what we did wrong and to steer clear of it the next time we are tempted. Bear the punishment. Pay the fines. Go to the classes. Walk through the darkness. God wants you free so you can minister to others going through this. He doesn't want you to love sin. He wants you to despise the very thought of it. He knows you can handle the chastening. He will not leave you nor forsake you. But you can't walk away from the process either. I know it's hard, but you will get through it. He began a good work in you. He did. Not you. And if he started it he will finish if we let him.

One verse many Christians love to quote is Jeremiah 29:11. Most of you can quote it without me writing it out. It's all about God's plans for good and not evil and for an expected end for his people. But what many people don't understand is that this scripture was a part of a prophesy foretelling God's judgement on his people for their disobedience. Letting them know that "yes, I'm sending you into captivity for a long time, and it's going to hurt, but when it is over, I will deliver you because you will have learned a very valuable lesson, and I love you."

Another example of this relationship between God and his people and the need to use suffering to discipline them is found in the book of Judges. After the death of Joshua, the people of God did not have one man that they looked to for leadership and government. As they attempted to govern themselves, they continued to fail miserably by disobeying God, which led to God's anger and punishment. Although at first, they tried to obey God, they often fell short and only partially obeyed, which caused them much trouble. Without the Godly leadership of Joshua and the elders who believed God and completely obeyed him the people fell into apostasy. This was due to the fact they refused to drive all their enemies out of the land they were called to inhabit. Instead, they chose to allow their enemies to stay and live amongst them as servants.

I often sit in judgment of the Children of Israel when I am reading the Old Testament and I see their actions. I sometimes shake my head and think, "how stupid," or "why would they do that?" Until I come to the realization that I have sometimes acted just like them. Do you always obey God completely? Have you ever partially obeyed God presuming that "God will understand?" Have you ever allowed your enemies to dwell with you; thinking, "they will serve me"?

The Bible says, "the weapons of our warfare are not carnal" (2 Cor. 10:4) because our enemies are not always carnal. Reading further in this verse, you will see that our weapons can cast down imaginations and thoughts and other nebulous enemies. To cast down imaginations you have to take your free-will and say no to any negative thought about God in your pain. Say out loud "God is sovereign, whatever he does is right no matter how it looks to me." That is what the Bible calls casting down imaginations and that is our job. Sometimes we have allowed those enemies in and have refused to cast them out because they "serve us." Oh yes, a terrible temper can serve you by making others do what you want them to do. A judgmental attitude can serve you by making you feel superior to others. Reveling can serve you by making you feel good. And what about stubbornness? Stubbornness can serve you by getting you what you want. Oh yes, we do have enemies that "serve us" that we need to destroy.

If we're using weapons and talking about warfare it means we're going to have to fight. We can't just lay down and take it, we have to fight. The good news is that God is Emmanuel. Which is "God with us." So, we are not fighting alone. Sometimes the fight may be just standing in all your armor. Not moving forward, but not moving backwards either. Just standing on the Word of God. And other times you will actively engage with the enemy.

But as in the days of the Judges, God in his faithfulness will help us to help ourselves by chastening us. In the book of Judges, the Bible records that the disobedience and apostasy of his children made God so angry that he delivered them over to their enemies to loot and plunder them so badly that they couldn't even withstand them. They were taken over by their enemies. The hand of the Lord was against them so much that every way they turned they felt his lash (kind of like when yo momma whooped you in a circle). The punishment was so harsh that it caused them to be extremely distressed (they couldn't sit down for a week). See Judges 2:14-15

If we hold onto our enemies like anger, stubbornness, and reveling, pretty soon they will take us over too. They will control us. Different versions of the Bible use various words to convey just how angry God was with his people. Words such as *furious*, *burned*, and *hot*. For example, they made God *furious*, or his anger *burned* against them, or his anger was *hot* against them. Are you getting a picture of an angry God? You don't want to make God angry. Yet, whenever they repented, God stepped in and rescued them after they cried out. He rescued them even though when their trouble eased up they returned to their evil. (See Judges 2:18) God truly loves us and has pity and great compassion on us. But it is possible to make him so angry that he allows us to suffer so that we will turn back to him. The proper response to this type of suffering is to repent and ask God for mercy:

> O Lord, correct me, but with judgment; not in thine anger, lest thou bring me to nothing.   Jeremiah 10:24

> O Lord, rebuke me not in thine anger, neither chasten me in thy hot displeasure. Have mercy upon me, O Lord; for I am weak: O Lord, heal me; for my bones are vexed.   Psalm 6:1-2

Things Happen

> And she went, and sat her down over against him a good way off, as it were a bow shot: for she said, Let me not see the death of the child. And she sat over against him, and lift up her voice, and wept. And God heard the voice of the lad; and the angel of God called to Hagar out of heaven, and said unto her, What aileth thee, Hagar? fear not; for God hath heard the voice of the lad where he is.   Genesis 21:16-17

Sometimes a series of events causes us to suffer. Sarah, Abraham's wife, had a slave named Hagar. Hagar found herself homeless, hungry, hurting, and helpless due to a series of unfortunate events. Sarah forced the slave to have sex with Abraham, Sarah's husband, to produce an heir in Sarah's name (this was legal in that culture). When Hagar found herself pregnant by her master (Abraham) she had an attitude change and despised Sarah. Sarah became angry with Hagar for this and began to treat her cruelly. Hagar decided to run away. Hagar really didn't have anywhere to go since she was pregnant and a slave. As a result, she just ran off into the wilderness and sat down by some fountain. This is where the angel found her and instructed her to return to her mistress and submit herself to her, and then the angel pronounced a blessing upon her and her child. And she did as the angel instructed.

When Hagar's son was a teenager, Sarah became pregnant and gave birth to her own son, as God had said. When she saw Hagar's son teasing her son (as children do) Sarah became angry and forced her husband to put Hagar and her son out. Abraham obeyed his wife as he was also instructed by the Lord, and sent Hagar and her son away. Again, we find Hagar in the wilderness without a plan, ready to give up, ready to die. An angel came to her again and helped her.

My question is, who's fault was it that Hagar had to suffer like this? Was it Sarah's fault for forcing her slave to become pregnant by her husband? Was it Hagar's fault for becoming haughty with her mistress? Was it Sarah's fault for forcing her husband to banish Hagar and her son? Was it Ishmaels's fault for teasing little Isaac? Was it Abraham's fault for listening to his wife in the first place? Why was Hagar a slave in the first place? How far back does blame go?

The first thing we love to do when we are suffering, or see suffering is to ask: "Who's fault was it?" Job's friends are the epitome of this phenomenon. They see Job is suffering, and yet they just have to find someone to blame. So, they sit with him and discuss the whys and the wherefores to come up with the exact wrong answer.

Sometimes the reasons we suffer are just complicated. It started a long time ago, and we were just a part of the story. Sometimes we are just collateral damage of someone else's story. Sometimes it just is. And we suffer. The Bible says: "Many are the afflictions of the righteous…" (Psalm 34:19a). Sometimes it's just because we are righteous.

The ability to reason causes us to seek an explanation for everything that happens. But for some things we will never receive an explanation on this side of Heaven. This is where faith comes in. Some people put their trust in science for explanations, but science has been proven wrong over and over again, yet people continue to believe because a pseudo explanation (to them) is better than no explanation. These people will say they don't have faith, but what they really mean is they don't have faith in God. Our sovereign God. Because for science to have been proven wrong so many times and yet they believe in it, that is the epitome of faith. But for those who have faith in the sovereign God and his Word we have the Bible. And even when our afflictions are complicated and we can't figure out where they came from, or who is at fault, we do "know that all things (really do) work together for good to them that love God, to them who are the called according to his purpose" (Romans 8:28, Emphasis mine). We know that God is a purposeful God and nothing that happens to us is arbitrary. God's purpose is always greater than our pain.

Chapter Four

Suffering From Our Own Foolish Decisions

> And David enquired of the Lord, saying, Shall I go up
> to the Philistines? wilt thou deliver them into mine
> hand? And the Lord said unto David, Go up: for I
> will doubtless deliver the Philistines into thine hand.
> 2 Samuel 5:19

Great leaders in the Bible didn't live their lives impulsively. When making life changing decisions, they sought wise counsel of the Lord. David knew that he couldn't go up against the enemy unless the Lord was with him. This Lord was the Lord of hosts (Jehovah Sabaoth). The God of the angel armies. David knew that if it was not in God's will that he defeat this enemy he would not be successful in spite of his reputation as a great warrior. David depended on God for direction and instruction and consequently in victory.

We often make life-changing decisions on our own and just expect God to bless them. One life-changing decision the devil uses repeatedly to destroy lives is marriage. The devil hates marriage and is so very glad to use it as his tool to destroy the faith of those who love God. We will make our own decision to marry someone who does not serve God. Not bothering to ask God about his opinion on the matter. Not asking "should I go up?" "Should I marry this person?" "Will we be able to stay together until death do us part?" Because there are people who go to church and are not serving God, and really God is the only one who knows who they are. Sometimes our friends and loved ones see it, but by the time they warn us, either we are too far gone to accept their opinion, or the person has isolated us from our friends and loved ones so that we fail to receive their opinion on the matter until it's too late.

While they are dating us everything is fine. Oh, we may have a few disagreements, but that is to be expected. We get past them. The devil will not allow them to show us anything that will hinder the marriage. We may see a few red flags, but we ignore them (they say love is blind). But after the vows are said and the honeymoon is over (sometimes even before the honeymoon is over) they begin to serve their father, the devil, bringing emotional pain and anguish into our lives. And we, being the Christian that we are, begin to pray to our father about the situation. We ask God to help us, to save our lives, or to deliver us, but the situation gets worse and worse. Then we begin to question our faith, the Bible, and our God. Is God good? Is he God? Should I get a divorce? Should I stay and wait on God? What should I do? And God is silent. Because you are asking the wrong questions. God is not for divorce. He will not tell you to divorce. It is totally against his will for the sanctity of marriage. But if you will ask the right questions God will guide your heart to safety in him.

One thing that is important to understand when dealing with people is that God gave us free-will and will not go against our free-will. We get to choose who we will serve. *"Know ye not, that to whom ye yield yourselves servants to obey, his servants ye are to whom ye obey; whether of sin unto death, or of obedience unto righteousness"* (Romans 6:16)? And so does everyone else on this earth. If our spouse chooses to serve the devil (and by not choosing to serve God they implicitly choose to serve the devil) there is no middle ground. Then they will do anything he tells them to do just to make your life miserable. You can pray for them to change, and God will honor your prayer and work in their life to bring about change. However, if they interpret God's signs differently and turn away from him instead of turning to him, God will not make them serve him against their free-will.

When it comes to other human beings, their outcomes are not in our hands. We can pray for them to want change, but ultimately the results are up to them because of free will. This is why it is so important for our spiritual well-being that we confer with God over their outcomes. As David did in all his battles, he conferred with the Lord concerning certain situations because only God knows the human heart and the ways of man. David could declare that God was faithful because he didn't place his trust in unreasonable expectations placed on God by him. David respected the proper order of things and understood the sovereignty of God. Once we settle God's sovereignty, that he is God and we are his people, we will not place unreasonable expectations on him but only expect what he tells us.

However, if we choose to place our unreasonable expectations on God, this is when anger towards him enters our spirit if we are not careful. So the question is, when we don't include God in our decisions and begin to suffer for it, why get angry at him? Here's what the Bible says about unreasonable expectations.

> For which of you, intending to build a tower, sitteth not down first, and counteth the cost, whether he have sufficient to finish it ? Or what king, going to make war against another king, sitteth not down first, and consulteth whether he be able with ten thousand to meet him that cometh against him with twenty thousand?
> Luke 14:28,31

Jesus said we are foolish if we make decisions without counting the cost. Part of counting the cost is by seeking good (Godly) counsel first. However, if you haven't sought good counsel, and find yourself in a predicament of a painful marriage. If you are afraid of getting a divorce because you love God, but you've been praying for your marriage and things have gotten worse, maybe it's time to change you. Maybe it's time to change your prayer. Maybe it's time to seek counsel of the Lord. Only God knows the end from the beginning. He knows the truth about your spouse and the truth about you. He knows how long you both will live and how much pain you can bear. He knows all about your suffering: "And the Lord said, I have surely seen the affliction of my people which are in Egypt, and have heard their cry by reason of their taskmasters; for I know their sorrows" (Exodus 3:7).

A better question to ask is *shall I go up?* God, will this person ever change? God, do I have the mental fortitude to withstand this level of pain until death? When God answers these questions from a pure and honest heart, remember he gave you free-will also and you get to choose whether or not you will stay. It's your choice. Always remember you have a choice. Sometimes we don't like either choice, but we still get to choose. And choice is empowerment. God empowers us to live our lives. But the greatest choice to make is to choose to believe that God is good, and that he loves you and wants what is best for you. But remember his ways are not our ways, so he may define "best" differently than we do.

And just because you chose God's best, don't expect it to be easy. Anything that's easy is not always the will of God. And everything that is hard is not always out of the will of God. God knew he was sending the children of Israel into a fight when he sent them into the promised land:

> And I am come down to deliver them out of the hand of the Egyptians, and to bring them up out of that land unto a good land and a large, unto a land flowing with milk and honey; unto the place of the Canaanites, and the Hittites, and the Amorites, and the Perizzites, and the Hivites, and the Jebusites.   Exodus 3:8

God knew the people who inhabited the land could fight and would fight for what they already possessed. However, that was nothing to God because he said, "*I have given it to you.*" It doesn't worry God when we come up against obstacles while doing what he told us to do. He's God. But it is up to us to ask. "Shall I go up?" Shall I start the business? Shall I start dating? Shall I look for a house? Shall I take this contract? Shall I? Shall I? Shall I go up? And when God answers, believe him.

Chapter Five
God as the Source of Suffering

But though He causes grief, yet will He be moved to compassion according to the multitude of His loving-kindness and tender mercy.
Lamentations. 3:32, AMPC

Throughout the pages of the Bible, we encounter examples of God becoming furious with his people for turning away from him. But then with as much compassion as he had anger, turning their sorrow into joy as they repent and turn back to him. Lamentations is known as *"the Book of Tears"* because the prophet Jeremiah weeps for the destruction of Jerusalem and feels the agony of the lash of God's anger personally. Jeremiah was obedient to God. He was his chosen prophet. God intimately knew him before he was born. Before his eyes ever saw the light of day, God knew him. Hence, it was very difficult for Jeremiah to comprehend the things he had to suffer along with the disobedient people to whom he was called to minister.

Read the third chapter of Lamentations. Feel the agony Jeremiah felt as he suffered along with God's chosen people. A people who had been grievously disobedient, yet, on the other hand, Jeremiah had not, but he still felt the rod of God's wrath. Jeremiah's complaint in this chapter mirrors the complaint of the descendants of Korah in the 44th Psalm. They were also struggling with unjust suffering. And even though they recognize God as the source of their suffering, they never blame God or accuse him falsely.

The Bible tells us that Job suffered unjustly and kept his integrity. Job was perfect and upright in God's sight, yet he suffered greatly.

But while he was going through it, he felt abandoned, ashamed, angry, and confused. Even when you've followed wholly after God's word you can still feel like God has forgotten you when you are suffering. Remember Elizabeth and her husband Zacharias? The Bible said about them that *"they were both righteous before God, walking in all the commandments and ordinances of the Lord blameless"* (Luke 1:6), and yet they suffered a long time. The Bible says that Elizabeth suffered reproach. And, what about this nameless prophet? This prophet served faithfully:

> Now there cried a certain woman of the wives of the sons of the prophets unto Elisha, saying, Thy servant my husband is dead; and thou knowest that thy servant did fear the Lord: and the creditor is come to take unto him my two sons to be bondmen.   2 Kings 4:1

And yet his wife is crying for welfare payments to keep her and her sons alive after God's faithful servant has died and left them alone.

What about Mary the mother of Jesus and her new husband Joseph? Smack dab in the middle of God's will for their lives, yet in her ninth month of pregnancy, the baby practically coming out, she has to go on a long journey to another city where her mother is not. As a matter of fact, the only family she had there was Joseph, a man who recently suspected her of being a cheater and was about to divorce her. People were talking about them, accusing them of being immoral. It's hot. The journey is long, and when they arrive there is no place to stay, not to mention a sanitary, safe place to have her baby. They end up in a stable. Even if the animals were gone, can you imagine the smell in that heat? Does this sound like blessed and highly favored to you? Does this sound like the life of a person who has found favor with God? What about Joseph? A just man? Yet after taking Mary as his wife he suffered right along with her. There are many other examples of Godly people in the Bible and present day who have suffered greatly from the hand of God and continued to worship, praise and honor him as their source of life. What was their secret? What did they know that we don't that can help us cope with trauma, pain, and suffering?

Emmanuel

> *Behold, a virgin shall be with child, and shall bring forth a son, and they shall call his name Emmanuel, which being interpreted is, God with us.*
> *Matthew 1:23*

Emmanuel doesn't just mean *God is with us*. It means so much more. The "El" part of his name means *might*. So not only is he with us, but he brings his might to the situation. As a result, as we turn to him in our distress we get to pull from his might. We get to trust in his might. He's a very present help and therefore we do not have to fear, be in distress, hide, cower or quake. We can stand boldly against our enemy.

> When thou goest out to battle against thine enemies, and seest horses, and chariots, and a people more than thou, be not afraid of them: for the Lord thy God is with thee, which brought thee up out of the land of Egypt. For the Lord your God is he that goeth with you, to fight for you against your enemies, to save you. Deuteronomy 20:1, 4

> For the Lord thy God walketh in the midst of thy camp, to deliver thee, and to give up thine enemies before thee; therefore shall thy camp be holy: that he see no unclean thing in thee, and turn away from thee. Deuteronomy 23:14

He is the fourth in the fire, he's the cloud between us and the enemy. He's the fire that goes in front to lead us. He makes the sun stand still so that we can finish the task. He's the wheel in the middle when life is turning us upside down round and round. He's the bread that falls from heaven when we are hungry. He's the one that comes riding on a cloud to deliver.

Even when I shouted and prayed for help, he refused

to listen". "From the bottom of the pit, I prayed to you, Lord. I begged you to listen. "Help!" I shouted. "Save me!" You answered my prayer and came when I was in need. You told me, "Don't worry!" You rescued me and saved my life." Lam. 3:8, 55-58, CEVDCI

When you reach bottom and God is there you learn. You learn not to fear the bottom. And this is trust. And this is where God wants us. God allows our struggles to draw us closer to him in a unique way. God will allow pain and suffering. And in those times, it seems like he is ignoring the fact that we are in pain. Yet he is Emmanuel. *God with us.* It's so easy to forget God is with us when we're suffering in the flames of affliction. We cry out and he doesn't answer. It seems like the heavens are silent, as if no one is there. It feels like you're going to perish. Then when you think it can't get any worse. It does. This time your cry is different. It is so desperate it cannot be ignored. And God shows up. He is there—*Jehovah Shammah.* When you have gone as low as you can go, God's arms can reach even lower. He won't let you be destroyed because *"The eternal God is thy refuge, and underneath are the everlasting arms: and he shall thrust out the enemy from before thee..." (Deuteronomy 33:27).*

God has always had big plans to dwell amongst his people and give them peace. To walk with them and talk with them and have relationship (Emmanuel). But because he also gave us free-will this did not happen. He said in Leviticus: *"If ye walk in my statutes, and keep my commandments, and do them; And I will set my tabernacle among you: and my soul shall not abhor you. And I will walk among you, and will be your God, and ye shall be my people" (26:3, 11-12).* The word "if" connotes choice, our choice. If you will read this entire chapter God is giving his people a choice to serve him, have relationship with him, and live in peace. But Peace does not mean the absence of conflict, it means victory over the enemy. Not being afraid or in want, that is the essence of peace.

Elisha's servant couldn't see God in a time of dire need for him and the prophet. Elisha knew God was with them and was going to act. However, his servant was anxious because he was in the dark. So, he went to Elisha in a panic and asked him *"What shall we do?" "And he (Elisha) answered, Fear not: for they that be with us are more than they that be with them. And Elisha prayed, and said, LORD, I pray thee, open his eyes, that he may see. And the LORD opened the eyes of the young man; and he saw: and, behold, the mountain was full of horses and chariots of fire round about Elisha"* (2 Kings 6:16-17).

When you need God but can't see him it's not because God isn't there. It's because your eyes are being blinded by the god of this world. Instead of being angry and turning away from God, ask him to open your eyes that you might see that he is for you. That he truly loves you and is prepared to fight your battles. Your enemy wants you to get frustrated, angry, and bitter and walk away from the only one that can help you. He doesn't want you to believe that God is good, and that he loves you with an everlasting love. That even if God is the cause of your grief, he also has compassion and a multitude of mercies waiting for you on the other side of your pain. To come to God all you have to do is believe that He Is, and that He Is a rewarder of them that diligently seek him. Your enemy wants to make you stop seeking God so that you won't get your reward for all the grief and pain you've experienced. But your only job is to turn away from the enemy and turn to God. In due time he will raise you up out of the pit and you will see his glory. 1 Peter 5:10 says, *"after you have suffered a while"* God will strengthen you, establish you and make you perfect.

What is *due time*? What is *a while*? Due time is a set time. God sets a time on our suffering; our job is to keep turning to him while we are going through, waiting on God to manifest his presence. Sometimes God is right there beside you like he was with the two disciples on the road to Emmaus. They were so sad that their hope had died, but they didn't know that Hope was walking with them and talking with them as they walked along in their pain. As they were talking with their hope about their pain, he was right there with them. Emmanuel. Until he opened their eyes and they understood. If you don't understand, tell God. He is right there with you; he is your living hope walking beside you. He waits to hear your cry.

"Underneath are the everlasting arms," there is no situation so deep that God can't get under it. His reach far exceeds ours. He can go lower than our lowest point in life, and he can reach higher than our greatest expectation. His everlasting arms can hold us in the midst of the direst situations. When we can't hold on any longer his everlasting arms are there. Psalm 90:2 says, *"from everlasting to everlasting, thou art God."* What confidence the writer exhibits! This psalm is attributed to Moses, the person God spoke to face-to-face. The person to whom God showed his hinder parts. Moses, that went to God every time the enemy came against God's people. And if you, like Moses, will turn to God instead of away from him when you are in trouble, even when it seems like he is not listening, you will become confident too.

Paul told the Corinthian's this very thing: *"Distress that drives us to God does that. It turns us around. It gets us back in the way of salvation. We never regret that kind of pain. But those who let distress drive them away from God are full of regrets, end up on a deathbed of regrets"* (2 Corinthians 7:10, MSG) It absolutely flummoxes the devil when we turn to God instead of turning away when he brings trouble. Look at Job. God bragged to the devil about him, and he will brag about you too.

Even after Jonah had disobeyed God, turned away from God and his instruction, when he got in trouble he knew enough to turn to the only one who could truly help him. He said:

"…I am cast out of thy sight; yet I will look again toward thy holy temple. When my soul fainted within me I remembered the Lord: and my prayer came in unto thee, into thine holy temple" (Jonah 2:4, 7). Jonah remembered God and God remembered him.

Turning to God is a choice we can make every time we are presented with evil. A choice God wants, begs us to make. He told the children of Israel: *"I call heaven and earth to witness against you today, that I have set before you life and death, the blessing and the curse. So choose life in order that you may live, you and your descendants…" (Deuteronomy 30:19, 20).* When you are feeling alone, and it seems as if God is ignoring your cry, always remember Immanuel. *"And they will call him Immanuel, which means 'God is with us" (Matthew 1:23, NLT)*. And then meditate on what it means to your life that *God is with us*. In light of any bad thing that has happened or will happen to you. Don't let your mind go to the negative. Think about what didn't happen and let your mind go into worship of God. You have a purpose in life. You are not here on this earth at this time arbitrarily. Don't ever forget that. Anxiety focuses on the negative that "could" happen. Faith focuses on the power of God to turn any negative into a positive.

What keeps you from turning to God in your times of trouble? Sometimes for some of us it's our unresolved anger with God. In times of suffering the biggest question that usually comes up is: "if God is good why is this happening to me? Why me?" This question usually fuels anger which has been boiling beneath the surface from other wrongs that have been perpetrated on us. It ignites a fuse of anger inside of our hearts to tempt us to turn against the God who loves us. The devil began slipping this seed of doubt into the minds of humans in the Garden. "If God is good, why can't you eat from that tree?" Our anger with God often stems from the fact that we don't believe he is good. Or we don't believe he is sovereign. The foremost question asked by nonbelievers is similar: "if there is a God why is there so much suffering in the world?" I believe this question is also fueled by the anger they feel at viewing or even experiencing suffering. Yet it's so hard for us to admit when we are angry with God. As if by not admitting it we're hiding it from him and he won't know. We convince ourselves that we can sneak by unnoticed and just stew in our anger a little while longer. Well, guess what? He knows. He knows and is just waiting for you to bring it to him so he can help you with it. Unresolved anger is like a splinter that was never removed. It sits below the surface, festering until you can no longer ignore it. It's painful and tender to the touch. And not only that, but it also alienates us from the only one who is able to fix it for us. That isolation then brings on a deeper sadness and opens us up to all sorts of other negative emotions. The next thing we know, we are swimming alone in a cesspool of negative emotions. The sad thing is, we don't have to experience this alone because he is with us.

I know this because I was there in that lonely cesspool. As a young wife and mother, I suffered a long time after my husband took my three children from me and gave custody to his sister. The pain of that loss was so devastating to me because it was my only goal in life to be a wife and mother. I had never aspired to any other station in life except wife and mother. Yet, I kept worshipping God. I learned to worship through my pain. But what I didn't know was that I needed to also bring that pain to my Father in Heaven. I needed to sit at his feet and cry my feelings and ask for his help in dealing with those feelings of loss, betrayal, powerlessness, anger, disillusionment, devastation, and shame. And probably a few more feelings that time will not allow me to name, but I think you understand. Yes, I prayed about the situation, but I didn't bring my feelings to him to let him heal those emotions while he was working on the problem. I didn't cultivate a close loving relationship with my Father in heaven that cares all about my hurts and pain. So those emotions had nowhere to go but to simmer beneath the surface of my consciousness and fester.

Until the explosion. When emotions are boiling beneath the surface, it only takes one thing to cause an explosion. My "one thing" was the army giving me orders to be stationed in Germany. A country so far away from my children that I despaired of life. I refused those orders and decided to go see my children one last time and then take my own life. What's that you say? Christians don't consider suicide? Have you read about Elijah, Jonah, Jeremiah, or even our beloved king David? They all went there. They wanted to die! And Jonah's desire to die stemmed directly from his anger with God. But thankfully when he wouldn't confront God with it, God confronted him, and they were able to talk about it. Because they had a close loving relationship.

How about Job? The Bible accounts that Job never charged God foolishly. But he did get angry with him. But the thing about Job, he knew where to take his anger. To the one he knew could do something about it. Now that's real worship. And that's real relationship. And you know what? Relationship is what God wants most from us. If all he wanted was worship, he had the angels. But he created man to have relationship. And in relationship, a healthy relationship, both parties get to talk. Both parties get to express their opinions and desires and needs and feelings. In a healthy relationship both parties listen to the other's views and takes the other's feelings into consideration. So don't let anger deter your relationship with God. That is a trick of the devil. He is the one whispering to you that God is mean, or that he doesn't care about you, and he doesn't care about your feelings.

Hebrews 4:6 says, our God commiserates with or feels compassion for us. Yes, God, all powerful, mighty, Alpha and Omega God. The God who exists because of himself cares about your feelings. Our God is full of compassion. And the *New Oxford American Dictionary* defines compassion as *"a sympathetic pity and concern for the sufferings or misfortune of others…."* And in the *Strong's Concordance of the Bible* the word *compassion* is made up of two words: *abundant and bowels*. The stomach in the human body is the center most place we feel emotions, and God made us in his image. Our God feels our pain so deeply. And guess what else? His compassion leads to mercy. In Lamentations 3:22, the passage declares:

"It is of the LORD's mercies that we are not consumed, because his compassions fail not."

If you don't believe God is good, read the following scripture over and over until it sinks in. He suffered and died for us. No one forced him. He did it willingly out of love. He looked into the future and saw our fate and said "I'll take the blame."

"I am the good shepherd: the good shepherd giveth his life for the sheep…. No man taketh it from me, but I lay it down of myself. I have power to lay it down, and I have power to take it again. This commandment have I received of my Father" (John 10:11,18).

So, I beg you not to continue simmering in emotions that are too much for you to handle on your own. Bring them to the compassionate God who really does love you and let him help you. The Bible says he will succor us. According to the *New Oxford American Dictionary* the word *succor* means: *"assist and support in times of hardship and distress."* It is a lie of Satan that keeps us from going to our

Father who loves us. Who do you want to believe, a liar who hates you and wants only to destroy you, or a God who loves you and is waiting to help you? It's your choice. But Deuteronomy 30:19 says *he wants us to choose him.*

The Fellowship of His Suffering

"I hear you, and maybe even agree. But how, you say? How do I, a human have that kind of relationship with God, a heavenly being?" First you get alone with him. Like going on a date. He said: *"be still and know that I am God" (Psalm 46:10a).* Be still. Turn off those distracting devices; the TV, your phone, the computer, and your I-pad. Set an atmosphere of solitude by closing the curtains and shutting the windows. Now think, and ask yourself, "what am I feeling?" About my problems, about my circumstances? Am I angry? What am I angry about? Who is the actual object of my anger? Admit your feelings to God out loud. I know you are supposed to enter his courts with praise and his gates with thanksgiving, but sometimes when we are angry, we can't think of anything to be thankful for. Don't worry, God will meet you where you're at. Bringing your anger to him instead of turning away from him *is* an act of worship. You are acknowledging him and his power to help. Have you ever loved someone but were mad at them at the same time? Have you ever been mad at someone, and they made you laugh? While you were still mad? As humans, understand that we are capable of feeling opposite emotions at the same time.

God knows, and cares. Don't make the mistake of thinking he is like us. His ways are not like ours, neither are his thoughts like our thoughts. If you have ever read the Bible, you have seen how much God can take. He put up with the shenanigans of his people over and over again. So don't believe the lie that if I'm angry with God if I come to him and tell him how angry I am, or even that I'm angry, he will smite me. He really hates smiting people. Lamentations 3:33-36 says God does not approve of nor enjoy afflicting humans and crushing us or perverting justice. But because of our negative bias (with a little help from the devil sometimes) we are inclined to believe it is

God bringing evil and pain on us for his pleasure. And it makes us angry. But let me tell you, if God brings or allows pain, it is always for a greater purpose. It may seem as if he is picking on us, or that he just hates us, but "au contraire" in that same chapter it says: *"For no one is abandoned by the Lord forever. Though he brings grief, he also shows compassion because of the greatness of his unfailing love" (31-32 NLT).*

You say, "what about war, famine, and racism?" I can't tell you why they happen, but I can tell you that because of offenses, I have learned the power of forgiveness. Because of poverty I have learned to depend on God to sustain me and he did. In famine I have eaten well. Through injustice I have learned mercy and grace. When the sun didn't shine and it began to rain and snow and storm, I learned to appreciate the sun. If life were sunny all the time, would we appreciate the sunshine? Or would we take it for granted? Yes, he allows pain and suffering, but he is with us in it and stands by to strengthen us and ultimately deliver us that he in the end, may get the glory. He said in Isaiah 43:7, that everyone that claims him as their God were created for his glory. And goes on to say in verses 20-21 that he made ways in the wilderness for them and even the wild animals would praise him because he provides water in the wilderness and rivers in the dessert for them. It is not pleasant to traverse the wilderness, but God is there, with us providing, making ways, strengthening us. Replenishing us. There's nothing more refreshing than water when you're thirsty. The desert is dry and hot but there is a God that sits high and looks low and sees you even when you feel like you are lost in a wilderness or struggling through a barren land. He is there because he cares.

Peter exhorted us to not be surprised, or "think it strange" when fiery trials come against us. He instructed that instead we should rejoice because it means that we are partakers in Christ's sufferings and that we would be glad later on. 1 Pet 4:12-13. "Partakers of Christ's sufferings;" or "fellowship of his suffering"; what is the fellowship of Christ's sufferings? Do you really know Christ if you have not suffered? Have you ever thought about what he suffered for you?

Did Christ feel this type of pain too? Even though he was sinless? Do you understand how he can be touched with the feelings of our infirmities? Hebrews 4:15 says, *"For we have not an high priest which cannot be touched with the feeling of our infirmities; but was in all points tempted like as we are, yet without sin"*. This scripture connotes that we will have infirmities. So why do we think it strange when the fiery trials come (1 Peter 4:12)? Why are we surprised that we suffer? When you fellowship with Christ in his suffering, you know that the Bible is real. There are plenty of scriptures that affirm that we will suffer. And as we fellowship with him in it, we realize the deep anguish he felt and we allow him to be our companion in our suffering.

When you have suffered you feel a deep connection to others who are suffering. You are able to hold their pain in a sacred silence that only you and they know. You can be a silent witness to the pain of others. You read the Bible differently. You feel the shame of the woman caught in adultery. You understand the loss of an only child. You experience the anguish of the man living in the tombs due to mental illness and demonic possession. And you know the loneliness Jesus felt as he prayed in the garden.

And he cometh unto the disciples, and findeth them asleep, and saith unto Peter, What, could ye not watch with me one hour? Matthew 26:40

Have you ever been in such deep anguish that you just wanted a witness to your pain? Jesus knew the disciples could not alleviate his pain. He knew there was absolutely nothing they could physically do to help him, but what he needed at that time was a witness. Yet he was denied even that. He had to bear his sorrow all alone. Jesus knows what it feels like to be emotionally abandoned. When your heart is breaking and everyone around you seems to be oblivious to your pain. I need to tell you from experience *Emmanuel* God is with us. God is witnessing our pain and knows exactly what to do with it. He has a purpose for it. He knows just how to take it and shape it into the vessel he can use at just the right time. So fellowship with him in your suffering. Sit with him in it. Invite him into your pain.

Yes, he felt this pain and yes, he loves you. Yes, he is with you in this time of suffering. Fellowship with him in it. Let your heart touch his. Let him hold you and succor you through it. The Bible uses the word *succor* which means, *assistance and support in times of hardship and distress*. Who better to do this than the one who also felt this pain but overcame it? He knows where it hurts, how it hurts, how long it will hurt, and just how to minister to that hurt. That specific hurt you're feeling right now. And he will bring you the type of comfort that only he can. Why? Because he is Emmanuel; God with us. He will never leave you nor forsake you. It may look like he has left you, and feel as though he has forsaken you, but if he said it shall he not perform it? Yes, there are plenty of scriptures that establish the fact that we will suffer. And there are also plenty of scriptures that promise he will deliver, rescue, help us escape, fix it, and heal us.

After This

The only way through suffering is to continuously turn to God in times of trouble, trials, or temptation. We have to practice turning to him and away from the temptation to get angry with him and therefore turn away from him. He has so much waiting for us on the other side. He has an *"after this"* for everything we go through if we will only turn to him and let him help us navigate the pain. The Bible says: *"**After this** lived Job an hundred and forty years, and saw his sons, and his sons' sons, even four generations. So Job died, being old and full of days" (Job 42:16-17)*. After he suffered, God came to him and comforted him. After Jesus suffered in the wilderness, angels came and ministered unto him. It's great news that God will comfort us. *"Blessed be God, even the Father of our Lord Jesus Christ, the Father of mercies, and the God of all comfort;" (2 Corinthians 1:3)*. God is absolute. He's the God of "all" comfort. There is no comfort like his, above his, or beside his. His comfort reaches every place you hurt. You can suffer through something that you feel "there's no way anyone can say anything that will make me feel better." And God will come along side you and bring a comfort that simply amazes you. Out of nowhere and out of nothing. You are simply comforted. *"Who comforteth us in all our tribulation, that we may be able to comfort* *them which are in any trouble, by the comfort wherewith we ourselves are comforted of God"* (2 Corinthians 1:4).

God has placed a gift inside all of us to help us cope with adversity. For some it may be a song, the gift to play a musical instrument, a sense of humor, the gift of love. We have to find that gift and explore its ability to bring comfort fully and share it with others who are hurting. In fact, God wants us to take that comfort we receive and use it to bring comfort to others. It sounds paradoxical but God has designed it to work. He is the designer of all comfort. And sometimes he chooses to use us mere mortals in his design. And that's a wonderful feeling, a type of comfort in itself. From God.

God gives us a ministry of reconciliation through suffering (see 2 Cor. 5:18-21). If Jesus knew no sin yet became sin for our sakes, to reconcile us to God, then why is it so hard for us to allow our suffering to be used to help someone else? God gave us the Bible, stories of people who faced the same issues we are facing, to assist us in our journey through pain and suffering. We can open the book and read about how Naomi lost her husband and two sons and journeyed through grief and bitterness, back to wholeness. We can read about David dealing with haters and family trauma. What about Samson who gave into his passion and lust over and over and yet was greatly loved by God? What about Gideon's identity crisis? Their stories are our stories. And our stories can be used in the same way, to help others understand that they are not alone in suffering, and that there is a God who loves them and is willing to walk through the fire with them if they will turn to him.

Chapter Six
God the Ultimate Power

For my thoughts are not your thoughts, neither are your ways my ways, saith the Lord. For as the heavens are higher than the earth, so are my ways higher than your ways, and my thoughts than your thoughts. Isaiah 55:8

Sometimes we suffer because we have unrealistic expectations of God stemming from not reading our Bible, misinterpreting the Bible, or hearing messages from "name it, claim it" false prophets. God said in Jeremiah if they are saying things he didn't say they are false prophets. His ways are higher than ours, and his thoughts are higher than the way we think. God is on a whole other level than us and he wants us to understand this. We look at suffering through human eyes and ask the question: "how can a good God allow such pain?" If you let him, God will teach you his way and you won't become bitter, or stay bitter when life doesn't look the way you want it to look. "*Shew me thy ways, O Lord; teach me thy paths. [9] The meek will he guide in judgment: and the meek will he teach his way*" (Psalm 25:4,9).

I have often speculated about the reasons behind the blood for remission of sin and suffering and pain. It made me think that maybe God was cruel, angry, sadistic, a lot like the wrathful God we see in the Old Testament, or that some preachers have preached about. But what if I'm wrong? I didn't create God, he created me. This is his world, and what if suffering and pain and shedding of blood mean something totally different to him? Colossians 1:20 says: *He made peace with everything in heaven and on earth by means of Christ's blood on the cross.* So, does this mean in God's realm peace comes from blood and suffering? We see violence, pain, and woe, but God sees peace. And being that he is our source (not the other way around), maybe we should try to see it his, way. Or at the very least stop accusing him of being unjust when we suffer or see suffering. It's a God thing, and no one really understands God; otherwise, he wouldn't be God. But know this, that God loves you with an everlasting love. And nothing can separate you from that love. In your personal time with the Lord read Romans 8:28-39.

God's intentions in suffering are often called to question. Whether from the person who is actually suffering, or people viewing suffering. But remember what sits between the tension of God's love for us and our suffering? His sovereignty. There is a story in the Bible that demonstrates sovereignty found in Matthew chapter 20. There is a landowner who goes out early in the morning to find laborers for his vineyard. He hires the first group and offers them a penny per day and they agree and begin working. Then in the afternoon he sees the need for more workers, and he goes out again and hires more and offers to pay them whatever is right, and they agree. He does this a couple more times until just an hour before the end of the workday ends, he hires more workers, and they agree to this pay scale.

When it is time to pay the workers, he pays everyone the same amount. Needless to say, the ones who worked all day were furious at the owner and demanded an answer as to why they were paid the same as people who only worked one hour. The owner simply informed them that it is his money, and they agreed to the pay before they accepted the job. Besides, he can do whatever he chooses with his money. When you are an owner of a house you can do anything you wish with that house. You can knock down walls, add on to it, paint, wallpaper, even sell it. It's yours. It belongs to you. When you own a car, it's yours. You can do whatever you wish with it (within the law). If you were an artist and created a piece of art, you could do whatever you wished with it. Why do we get mad at the creator of this world for not running it the way we want him to? Psalm 115:16 says: *"The Lord has kept the heavens for himself, but he has given the earth to us humans"* (CEV). God gave the earth over to humans. After the fall of man evil invaded the earth. Mankind began to choose evil over good and then blame God for all the tragedies. What gives us the right to blame God or get angry with him for anything he allows to happen in his world? *"The heavens are thine, the earth also is thine: As for the world and the fulness thereof, thou hast founded them. The north and the south thou hast created them:" (Psalm 89:11-12a)*. It all belongs to him.

Many have turned away from God because they blamed God or became angry with him, or viewed him as cruel, punitive, vengeful, angry, or some equivalent word that throws him into a negative light. But just because you view something bad happening to you or someone else from this side of heaven doesn't mean you know the whole story. You cannot tell God's intentions unless you believe you created God. Then my question to you would be: "did you create God? Or did God create you?" If you created God, does that mean you are the highest power on earth? If you are the highest power on earth, why aren't you stopping all the evil that is prevailing? If you created God, then you are responsible for what goes on in the world. If you are the ultimate power, then you should be the one to alleviate suffering and evil. By the way, did you create evil and suffering also? But if God created you then he is the ultimate power. He is sovereign and whatever he does is right. Even when we don't understand. He is all powerful and can do whatever he chooses. The prophet Habakkuk asked God these questions. Why God, why? Why am I seeing evil prevail on earth? Why don't you do something about it? Aren't you all powerful? Don't you see it? But instead of turning away in anger from the only one who could give him the answer he chose to wait on an answer from God. He said: *"I will climb up to my watchtower and stand at my guardpost. There I will wait to see what the Lord says and how he will answer my complaint"* (Habakkuk 2:1, NLT). And he waited. When faced with doubt, fear, and even anger and outrage at our experience of evil, our best bet is to turn to the one who created us. Ask him about his intentions, then wait for an answer. No matter how long the wait. In the meantime, find out what your part is in making it better.

Jesus instructed his disciples in Matthew the sixth chapter, what is commonly called the "Lord's Prayer" to pray for God's kingdom to come and his will be done on earth as it is in heaven. This instruction connotes that heaven is very different than earth; and that as his followers we can ask him to change things on earth through the power of prayer. That's it. That's our part. Just be "putty in his hands" and let him worry about the big stuff.

Personally, I'm glad that I am not God and am not ultimately responsible for this whole universe. I am glad to just be clay. I am not interested in being the potter and having the responsibility of a whole human race. I am so glad that there is someone bigger than you or I to whom we can turn when evil seems to prevail or when life seems purposeless. Having a higher being, something outside myself that is greater than me or any other being is so comforting to me and is what gives my life purpose. I'm glad he has a plan and a purpose that is greater than my suffering. I may not always understand what he is doing, but because I know his character, I am confident I will come out victorious.

God's Character

> *Martha said to Jesus, "Lord, if only you had been here, my brother would not have died. But even now I know that God will give you whatever you ask.*
> *John 11:21-22, NLT*

Sometimes we vacillate between faith and doubt, but that's okay. However, when we know his character we will choose faith. This is what Martha knew. This is why she said "even now" I know you can fix this; I know you can do anything. You're connected to God, and you love us. Even though you were late, it's not too late. You're still good! You're still God! You never fail.

Jesus declared to his disciples, specifically to Thomas: "*I Am the way the truth and the life" (John 14:6)*. Jesus is the truth. Jesus is the Word. Therefore, the Word of God is the truth. The Word of God will make us free because in the Word lies the truth about God's character-that he is good. When we know God's character, we can repose in it. Like an easy chair, or a recliner. Not a care in the world, because we know it's good because God is Alpha and Omega. Knowing God's character brings about a confidence that cannot be shaken. We are sure that if he sets it in motion, he will finish it. We know this through relationship with him.

Martha and her sister Mary had a close relationship with Jesus. Once when he came to their home for dinner, Martha asked him to make her sister help her with the serving and clean-up. Martha felt like she could ask Jesus anything. And guess what? She could; and so can we if we cultivate a close relationship with him. Now, being able to ask Jesus anything doesn't mean we can make him do it. Jesus essentially told Martha no. But the point is, because she had relationship with him, she felt comfortable asking. She knew his character and was able to take the slight rebuke from him. Because she knew his character, she understood that his no didn't mean he hated her, or wasn't going to be her friend anymore. It was just a no, nothing more. Sometimes when we get a no from God, if we don't know his character we can be left feeling as if God hates us, or no longer cares about what happens to us. But when we have an understanding of his character, we can cope with anything life brings, even when he says no.

"The name of the Lord is a strong tower: the righteous runneth into it, and is safe" (Proverbs 18:10).

The Hebrew word for *name* can also be translated as *character*. So, we could say: *"the character of God is a strong tower and the righteous can find safety there."* Because we know God's character we can lean and depend on him when our world seems to be falling apart. According to the *Random House Unabridged Dictionary*, the word *character* means: *"the aggregate (or combination) of features and traits that form the individual nature of some person or thing."* There is a combination of traits that inform us about the nature of God and cause us to be able to trust and believe in him.

The first trait is Holiness. God is *Holy*. Which is to say he's morally pure, divine, and supernatural. He is above anything that is natural. His abilities far outweigh our abilities. He's above us and his ways are not our ways (Isaiah 55:8). This is why when we are in trouble and we can't see any way out, God is still able to make a way, because he is holy and powerful.

Which brings me to the next characteristic of God: *omnipotence* (Rev 19:6). God is all powerful. He holds all power in his hands. There is nothing too hard for him. And when we get in trouble if we turn to him, and he brings his power into our situation we don't have anything to worry about. He is *Almighty*. In *Thayer's Greek Lexicon*, *almighty* is defined as: *The one who holds sway (the power to cause something to change) over everything*. In Revelation 1:8, God introduced himself in a proclamation: *"I am Alpha and Omega, the beginning and the ending, saith the Lord, which is, and which was, and which is to come, the Almighty."* "Hello, I Am God. I Am here. I was here. And I'm always going to be here." And let's not forget every time God says "I Am" it's not like when just anyone says it. He's the "I Am" that Moses met. The *Self-Existent One*. God-all-by-himself-don't-need-no-help One. He's saying, "I don't want any confusion as to who I Am". So I repeat "Alpha, Omega, and if you don't understand that, beginning, end. Got it? Ok". God knows how to reveal himself. When he wants to. If he doesn't, he can be such a mystery. But when he does, it is so glorious it will cause you to fall to your knees in worship.

God is faithful, merciful, and full of compassion. Lamentations 3:22-23 says: *"It is of the Lord's mercies that we are not consumed, because his compassions fail not. They are new every morning: great is thy faithfulness"*. The word *great* doesn't begin to convey the faithfulness of God. You may wonder what faithfulness has to do with suffering. It has everything to do with suffering. If we know we can trust and depend on a compassionate merciful loving God, that every day when we wake up, he is going to faithfully provide the mercies we need for that day. I don't know about you, but this knowledge brings peace to my soul. Every day he faithfully gives us another chance (a new mercy) to get it right. So many days, so many mercies! Because he is merciful and compassionate, he wants us to get it right. Consequently, if I live another day, I know things can change.

I have personally experienced the faithfulness of God in my suffering. There was a time in my life I didn't want to live another day, because I was going through a terrible time of suffering. I felt that if I could just die the suffering would stop. Suicidal thoughts are from the pits of hell. The enemy of our soul knows that God's mercies are new every morning. He knows that if we can just get up and be alive God is faithful, and that situation will change. That God won't let us be consumed, devoured, or swallowed up by our pain (Daniel was not consumed by lions. The Hebrew boys were not consumed by the fire. Peter was not consumed by the sea, and I was not consumed by my situation). The enemy knows that God has relief waiting on the other side of our suffering, because his compassions never fail. And not just relief, but great joy, and power, and the ability to comfort others with the comfort we were comforted with.

In Deuteronomy 30:19, God urges us to *"choose life that both thou and thy seed may live."* Where there is life there is hope. We must live to see our children, and our children's children live out their purpose. There are other people after you who need to live too. Just your being alive is a testimony to God's enemies that he won't fail. God has a great plan however, pain and suffering are a part of that plan. Those who press through the pain and suffering live to walk out that plan and become a part of the greatest story ever told.

GOD IS LOVE

God is love; and he that dwelleth in love dwelleth in God, and God in him" 1 John 4:16a

Not only does God have love for us, he *is* Love. God's love is everlasting (Jer. 31:3). His love is unfailing. There are 121 Bible verses about unfailing love in the *New Living Translation* of the Bible and many of them tell how God *lavishes* unfailing love on his people.

When you are suffering it is very hard to remember that you are loved. This is why I am so grateful for the Bible, Bible apps, and Bible websites. God's love is always at our fingertips. We can go to the word of God anytime of the day or night and read about or listen to scripture after scripture on how much he loves us. I encourage you, if you are suffering, go to the pages of the love letter he wrote to us and bask in his unfailing love. Just see how affectionately God speaks to his people. Even though they kept turning away from him and serving other gods, yet, in loving kindness and tender mercies he kept calling to them, tenderly loving them.

David declared God's goodness and unfailing love over and over in the Psalms. *Surely goodness and mercy shall follow me all the days of my life:" (Psalm 23:6).* And Jesus verified that he would be with us, *"But after that I am risen, I will go before you into Galilee" (Mark 14:28). "...and, lo, I am with you alway, even unto the end of the world. Amen" (Matthew 28:20).* So, if goodness and mercy are following me and Jesus goes before me, and he is with me, why should I fear? I don't have to be startled or rattled. I don't have to dread or have evil forebodings. I know that God is for me. When fear and evil forebodings come against us, or when we are suffering and just don't understand, we have to settle in our minds that God is for us and that he is good. We must believe that anything that he allows to come against us or happen to us is only for our good.

There is a reason or lesson somewhere in the problem. And don't let the devil intimidate you with what could happen. Remember, it is God that sets the parameters of his children's suffering. We learned that in Job. And in Ecclesiastes *"When times are good, you should be cheerful; when times are bad, think about what it means. God makes them both to keep us from knowing what will happen next" (Ecclesiastes 7:14 CEVDCI).* So, instead of dwelling on the problem I should meditate on his goodness and talk to him about the reason or lesson in the situation. If I ever said it once I will say it a thousand times: *what God wants from us is relationship!* He wants us to bring our troubles and problems to him. He wants us to talk to him and commune (communicate intimately) with him about it. He wants to be our hero. *"For the eyes of the Lord run to and fro throughout the whole earth, to shew himself strong in the behalf of them whose heart is perfect toward him" (2 Chronicles 16:9a)*. Unfortunately, in order for him to show himself strong on our behalf, there has to be a significant problem in our life.

Job declared: *"Though he slay me yet will I trust him"(Job 13:15)*. In spite of his terrible suffering Job knew deep down inside that God loved him and was good. Even though Job lived before Jesus died for us, something inside of him informed him that God was trustworthy. The way to live in peace through suffering is to resolve the question in your heart of God's love and goodness every time it lifts its ugly head. Resolve that God is for me, his banner over me is love. God "so" (extremely) loved the world, I am a part of that world. He extremely loves me. How can you doubt a love that is so extreme he gave up his only begotten son for sons and daughters that didn't even know him? We were adopted. Let that sink in.

God is a Good Father

If a son shall ask bread of any of you that is a father, will he give him a stone? or if he ask a fish, will he for a fish give him a serpent? Or if he shall ask an egg, will he offer him a scorpion? If ye then, being evil, know how to give good gifts unto your children: how much more shall your heavenly Father give the Holy Spirit to them that ask him?
Luke 11:11-13

Why are we so quick to believe that God is evil, mean, out to get us, when trouble comes in our lives? God is good. He only wants good for us. He is not out to get us. He has good plans for us and not evil as he told Jeremiah (29:11). So, when the bad times come, and they will (see Job 14:1) and the accusations against God come to mind, pause and calmly think about this. What have I asked him for? Did I ask him? If you have asked him for something and what you're getting doesn't look anything like what you asked for first consider, was I specific? God is a specific God. Did I ask? Sometimes we think we have asked when actually we haven't even spoken to him. God knows your thoughts, but he answers prayers.

God Listens to Our Prayers

> *"For He has not despised nor detested the suffering of the afflicted; Nor has He hidden His face from him; But when he cried to Him for help, He listened."*
> *Psalms 22:24, AMP*

The King James Version says "when he cried unto him, he heard." God really does hear our cries. Psalm 34:15 says God's ears are open to the cries of the righteous. And the 17th verse says God hears and delivers the righteous out of all their troubles.

God heard Daniel's prayer (Daniel 10:12). God heard Zacharias (Luke 1:13). God even heard the prayer of a Gentile, a Roman centurion no less (Acts 10:30-31). God heard Hannah's prayer. Even though Hannah was actually loved, her circumstances made her feel opposite of that. She wasn't able to feel in her emotions that she was loved. She was married to a rich man that loved her. But she had a situation. Have you ever had a situation that changed your emotions? (A mental illness diagnosis, a chronic disease, abuse, illicit attractions, a horrible boss, haters, a toxic work environment, unmotivated employees (if you're a boss), financial situations, lack, barrenness, to cover just a few).

Hannah was barren. What does it feel like to be barren? In a culture where a woman's worth was measured by her ability to have children. On top of being barren she also had a hater living in the home with her. Her husband Elkanah's other wife, Peninnah. *"So Peninnah would taunt Hannah and make fun of her because the Lord had kept her from having children (1 Sam 1:6, NLT).* This happened year after year. Haters will always try to keep your faults in front of you. They have to make you feel small so they can feel better about themselves. What must that have been like for Hannah? And if the woman openly taunted Hannah did her children also? And why did Elkanah allow this to continue if he loved her so much? He had to know. What's it like when people say they love you but only give you the kind of love they want to give? They give you the: "I bought you this house, I pay the bills but I'm angry with you all the time" kind of love.

Hannah was in deep anguish, crying bitterly as she prayed to the Lord." (1 Samuel 1:6, 10, NLT). When did Hannah pray? After things got really ugly. It took years for this to fester and grow really ugly. The Bible gives us a clue that the situation had gone on for a long time because it states that her rival had at least four children. The Bible says her husband gave portions to all her (rival's) children and she had girls and boys (plural) also it says her rival's children were old enough to go sacrifice. So, it's safe to say that Hannah had suffered a long time in this situation.

How did she pray? Fervently! Her problem came from the Lord, but she turned to him instead of away from him. *"The Lord had shut up her womb" (1 Sam 1:6)* which gave her rival cause to taunt her and showed how insensitive her husband really was. And then got her falsely accused by Eli the priest. Yet she pressed through all of that to turn to God. Sometimes we have to press through a lot of stuff, including our feelings to go to God in prayer. But we can continue turning to him in our distress because we know he hears our prayers.

When we suffer and are in deep anguish the proper place to go, the best place to go is to the Lord. He is the one who can change things. When we suffer our prayer should be "thank you Lord for drawing me closer to you through suffering". But so often we let our anguish cause us to become bitter against the only one who can actually help. Instead of becoming bitter we should take our anguish to him and ask him to *"Make us glad according to the days wherein thou hast afflicted us, and the years wherein we have seen evil" (Psalms 90:15)*.

Hannah didn't know her story was going to be in the Bible. She didn't know that God was using her situation to get glory. She didn't know that the thing that God birthed from her pain was going to be one of the greatest prophets that ever lived. She didn't know that her situation would bring forth the anointing for the first king of Israel. She didn't know that she had so much greatness in her. But what she did know was that: *God is good, God hears prayers, and "The effectual fervent Prayer of the righteous availeth much."* (See James 5:16) The Bible reports that Hannah had five more children after having Samuel. And her first son Samuel was one of the greatest prophets of the Old Testament. Not only that, he had a relationship with his mother and father after he was grown because the Bible reports that Samuel's home was in Ramah (The city his parents lived in) when he was grown. So, God did make Hannah glad according to the years she suffered.

Chapter Seven

Yeah, But I'm Angry!

I understand that God is sovereign. I get it. I know that I need to get with his program, but I am still angry. I became a Christian because I thought God loved me. I didn't sign up for this! Well, first of all, "you kinda did." There are so many scriptures in the Bible warning us that if we follow Christ, we will have a cross to bear. The Cross equals suffering. But those scriptures aren't really helpful when you're in the thick of it. When life is beating up on you, and you can hardly catch your breath before another problem arises out of nowhere. I totally get it! It's during one of those times I wrote the following poem:

THERE WILL BE DAYS LIKE THIS
By: Cynthia Gibson-Dyse

When you don't want to live, but you don't want to die.

You can't give up, but you don't want to try.

Everything's wrong; nothing seems right.

And there seems to be no end in sight.

Keep pressing on, it won't be long.

When friends seem so far away,

and life gets tougher day by day.

When you want to sit around and cry

because everything good seems to pass you by.

Keep pressing on, it won't be long.

It won't be long til you're looking up,

and everything good will fill your cup.

When friends come back to help your plight;

and the end suddenly comes back in sight.

And you'll say to yourself when the day is done,

"I'm glad I kept trying, I'm glad I held on!"

Yes, there will be days that the whole world seems to come crashing down on you. Sometimes many days in a row. Sometimes days turn into weeks, and weeks turn into months, and months turn into years, and still there is no relief. In those times I have learned to preach to myself. I want to share with you some of the things I preach to myself when I suffer that help me align my will to his, and I hope they will help you as you grapple with whatever you are going through.

GOD CREATED ME; I DID NOT CREATE HIM

"For we are God's masterpiece. He has created us anew in Christ Jesus, so we can do the good things he planned for us long ago"
Ephesians 2:10, NLT

If God created me, and I did not create him, then that means he is the ultimate authority over my life, not me.

> Thou art worthy, O Lord, to receive glory and honour and power: for thou hast created all things, and for thy pleasure they are and were created.
>   Revelation 4:11

> For by him were all things created, that are in heaven, and that are in earth, visible and invisible, whether they be thrones, or dominions, or principalities, or powers: all things were created by him, and for him.
> Colossians 1:16

God being the creator of all makes him sovereign. Which means he has the absolute power to do whatever he pleases. This is the reason I turn to God when I suffer. I know that he created me and therefore knows what I can take. Sometimes it feels like I can't take it, but I know God wouldn't create a masterpiece only to destroy it. When the things that I am feeling and the things I know don't line up, I lean towards what I know. The word of God is truth, and not one word from him will ever fall to the ground.

I Am Bought with a Price

"He created me, then after I was sold into sin he bought me back from sin" (redemption). *"...the church of God, which he hath purchased with his own blood" (Acts 20:28)*. Peter delves deeper into this subject in 1 Peter 1:18-20. In his letter to early Christians who were scattered due to persecution. He wanted to remind them in their suffering that their lives were empty before they received Christ, and that they were in this condition through no fault of their own, but this emptiness was inherited from their ancestors. He wanted them to realize the value of their salvation which was purchased with the blood of Jesus, which was much more precious than any earthly element they could possess. He stresses to them that Jesus' blood was very precious and should be valued greatly because he was the only sinless, spotless Lamb of God that was chosen by God to take away our sins, so that we could be saved from eternal damnation. Jesus was "Called to Suffer and Chosen for Greatness."

When I think about the price God paid to redeem my life back from the sin I was sold into, it takes my breath away. He left his throne and all the glory of heaven, to come to earth to pay the price just to obey his own rule. He is God. He could have just changed the rules if he had wanted to, but he wanted to know us intimately, so he put on flesh and became one of us to satisfy the need of a sacrifice to himself. He became his own sacrifice. As Abraham told Isaac *"God will provide Himself a lamb" (Gen. 22:8)*. And he did. He came down to earth and became the sacrificial lamb for your sins and mine. I don't know about you, but when someone makes a sacrifice for me, I feel loved. Not only did God make a sacrifice for me, but he became that sacrifice. 1 Corinthians 6:20a says it this way: *"for God bought you with a high price…(NLT)*. We were purchased by God with love and because he loved us that much, we love him. When I think about how much he loved me I can't help but say yes to his will. I bow before his majesty. (Royal power, dignity, stateliness, and awesome beauty).

My Life is not My Own

"What? know ye not that your body is the temple of the Holy Ghost which is in you, which ye have of God, and ye are not your own (1 Corinthians 6:19)? I don't belong to myself. I belong to God. Since I belong to him, he can do whatever he pleases with my life and I am okay with it. I am the clay and he is the potter. *"You have everything backward! Should the potter be thought of as clay? Should what is made say of its maker, "He didn't make me"? Should what is shaped say of the one who shaped it, "He doesn't understand"? (Isaiah 29:16 CEB)*. God is saying, "Don't get it twisted, I created you, you did not create me." When you create something, as the designer you are the one that decides its use. The thing has no say in how it is used. But as God's beloved creation I don't mind yielding my life to his service.

To me, it is an honor to let God use my life as he sees fit. I love belonging to him and living in him. As Paul said, *"For in him we live, and move, and have our being" (Acts 17:28a)*. Paul was preaching to a group of Athenian idol worshippers who were afraid of offending any God, so they had set up an altar to *The Unknown God*. Our every movement and our very existence, even our identity is all wrapped up in our creator. Paul goes on to say that we are also God's children. I know as a child I didn't mind allowing my parents to shoulder all the responsibility while I went outside to play. And living in Christ, I don't mind letting him shoulder all the responsibility of my complex life while I follow his commands and just be his. I gladly turn the final say-so over to him because I belong to him. God knows how to teach great lessons through pain. Lessons that we would never be able to learn otherwise, without the pain. He knows the right pressure to put in the right places that will make us turn to him. And in turning we are shaped on his potter's wheel.

It Came to Pass

For our light affliction, which is but for a moment, worketh for us a far more exceeding and eternal weight of glory (2 Cor. 4:17). Suffering in light of eternity is only for a moment. In this life all we have are moments, and memories of those moments. Our moments may be painful, but we can make our memories of those moments joyful. If you can look back on each moment and know that in between each painful moment I laughed, then suffering has no power over you. You have gained dominion over suffering. Even if you didn't laugh before because life was so painful and you didn't know what joy or laughter was, you can start now. And the joy of today can mitigate if not totally eradicate the pain of yesterday. When you are in great pain, you can walk in the knowledge that the pain you are feeling in the moment will pass and only become a memory one day. It can be a painful memory, or it can just pass away like every other painful time has passed. We don't have to hold on to the pain. Sometimes we just have to survive long enough to see God turn our mourning into dancing and our sorrows into joy. The Bible says *to agree with thine adversary quickly*. Well, sometimes our adversary isn't a person, it's a feeling, a situation, a thought. Agreeing with it doesn't mean you agree to it staying on a permanent basis. It means don't fight it. Let it be what it is. For now. It's here for a moment. We have to sit through the nasty, ugly feelings and wait until our change comes. It will come if you hold on. Last through the moments. Knowing they are just moments. Even though it seems like an eternity while we are in it. If you can get through one moment you can get through ten. And if you can get through ten you can get through twenty. Before you know it, the day has passed, and you find yourself walking in the light of change.

HIS GRACE IS SUFFICIENT

My grace is sufficient for thee: for my strength is made perfect in weakness. Most gladly therefore will I rather glory in my infirmities, that the power of Christ may rest upon me. Therefore I take pleasure in infirmities, in reproaches, in necessities, in persecutions, in distresses for Christ's sake: for when I am weak, then am I strong.
2 Corinthians 12:9-10

One of the main reasons we suffer is Lack. Lack of love, lack of finances, lack of health, lack of necessities, lack of things we want. Any kind of lack can be the root of suffering. But I gladly suffer lack, because sometimes my lack is God's provision. Through my lack God is providing me with an arsenal of faith. Because when I have lack and turn to God, I seek him and what his word says. And I begin to see him and life in a different way, and I learn that he is all I need. That his grace is sufficient for me. Paul suffered from a lack of comfort. He was speaking of a thorn in his flesh that he had prayed to God to remove. But when Paul leaned into the grace of God, he was able to change his thinking even though the situation did not change. God told him it wouldn't, but Paul was able to endure simply because of God's grace. God knows how to make us stand in spite of our afflictions. Paul, instead of being angry that he was not able to do everything he wanted to do due to this "thorn", gives glory to God. He is able to do more for God with a thorn in his flesh than most people can do without. He traveled all over, established churches, and helped them to thrive through continuous ministry through letters, and training, mentoring, and then sending other ministers to them. And you need to know that God is still on his throne making things happen through his people. Whatever your thorn in the flesh is, know this, if God be for us who can be against us? Or what thorn can keep us down? God is able to move through depressed people, people with bipolar disorder, people with diabetes, divorced people, married people, never been married people. Whatever "thorn" you have, God is still able to use you to his glory because his grace is sufficient. Grace is favor bestowed on the undeserving, but it is motivated by delight. The giver of grace has to have a generous character. God has a generous character. When we are suffering it may seem as if grace is far from us, but it's really just a prayer away. Remember, Paul prayed three times, and Jesus prayed three times in the garden before going to the cross, so don't give up if you don't receive it the first time you pray, pray, and pray again.

I Belong to God. He has a Plan for My Life

"for you are a chosen people. You are royal priests, a holy nation, God's very own possession. As a result, you can show others the goodness of God, for he called you out of the darkness into his wonderful light."
1 Peter 2:9 NLT.

"all things were created by him, and for him" Col 1:16b.

To be chosen, means to be specially selected. To be specially selected by God, "The God" is an awesome privilege. God created us for his own purpose. We are his possession. I am happy to be a possession of a good God. If I belong to God, a good God, I am happy to do the things that please him and not myself. In every love relationship the time will come when one has to choose between doing what makes "self" happy or what will make the other person happy. When you genuinely love someone, you really want to do the things that will bring them happiness, bring a smile to their face. And sometimes it will be to the detriment of your own comfort, but you do it anyway. That is how I feel about belonging to God. I am fully persuaded that he is good and that he loves me. So, when I am suffering and I don't understand, I can always lean into the fact that he is good, he chose me, and he has a plan. When I think about how he brought me out of the darkness that my life was and turned his light on my life, I'm ok with the difficulties, pain, and inconveniences I face. I rest in the fact that he's "got me," and a willingness to show others his goodness arises inside of me.

IT'S FOR HIS NAME'S SAKE

"... he leadeth me in the paths of righteousness for his name's sake." (Psalms 23:3). The word "name" in this scripture denotes honor. Other versions translate *"for His name's sake"* as *"bringing honor to his name"* NLT or *"for the sake of his good name"* CEB.

Luke 21:17 says we will be hated for his name's sake. In Acts 9:16, God told Ananias that he would show Saul (Paul) what great things he would suffer for his (God's) name's sake. Because of my love for God, I don't mind doing anything to bring honor to him. He saved my life. Not just my life, my soul. I want to be able to do anything he asks me to do if it will bring honor to him.

GOD IS FOR ME

"What shall we then say to these things? If God be for us, who can be against us?" Romans 8:31. God is the one true and living God, the Supreme Being, why should I fear anything if he is on my side? I am more than a conqueror through him. And David said this twice: *I trust in God, so why should I be afraid? What can mere mortals do to me? (Psalm 56:11 NLT)*, and *The Lord is for me, so I will have no fear. What can mere people do to me (Psalm 118:6, NLT).* When we are in the midst of suffering and pain, sometimes it's hard to believe God is for us. It can even be hard to believe that he is good, or for that matter that he even exists. But when I turn to the word of God, I can't help but believe. We have a great cloud of witnesses that even in sorrow and pain God is on our side and wants us to win. He even orchestrates the win for us. We just have to hold on and believe. You have to believe God is good through your suffering. Not only believe it but tattoo it on your brain. (Exodus 13:16, Deuteronomy 6:8, 11:18).

"For the thing which I greatly feared is come upon me, and that which I was afraid of is come unto me" (Job 3:25). Sometimes the thing we greatly fear is the same thing that we greatly hate, but it comes anyway. We may do everything in our power to prevent it, avoid it, to fight against it but it comes upon us anyway. What do you do? I was a person that hated divorce. Yet I have been divorced twice. I fought

hard against it. Did everything I knew to prevent it. And yet here we are, two divorces later. It brought with it depression, great condemnation, and all manner of other evil into my life. So, you may ask what happened? I wrote this book. I made it through the pain, the agony, the depression and feelings of defeat. I survived the furnace of affliction. And like the proverbial Phoenix, I rose up from the ashes and I am walking in God's Grace and mercy every day because God is for me.

When Bitterness Sets In

"But she said, "Don't call me Naomi; call me Bitter. The Strong One has dealt me a bitter blow. I left here full of life, and GOD has brought me back with nothing but the clothes on my back. Why would you call me Naomi? God certainly doesn't. The Strong One ruined me." (Ruth 1:20-21, MSG)

If we are not careful to guard our heart, we can become bitter through suffering. We can start off delighted in God and end up in bitterness. This is what happened to Naomi. The name Naomi means *my delight* in Hebrew. Yet after suffering many tragedies, she changed it to *Mara* which means *bitterness*.

All Naomi could see was what she didn't have. She let her circumstances dictate her feelings. In the popular culture, we would say "she was in her feelings." Naomi had experienced great loss. She had lost her husband, and her two sons. It was a dangerous situation to be in in those days, to be a woman with no man to protect and provide for you. Sometimes, when our circumstances are threatening, we can let fear dictate the rest of our emotions and let negativity reign in our soul. When negativity begins to reign, it makes us forget everything positive in our lives and we can become bitter. Bitterness is an ugly place to dwell. It blinds us to everything that is right. Naomi wasn't bereft of everything. Even though she was in one of the worst positions a woman in that day could find herself in, all was not lost. Naomi still had plenty left, but bitterness would not allow her to see it. Naomi was in mourning. As a matter of fact, she had passed mourning and entered into grief.

No matter how dire our circumstances get, God always leaves us with a remnant. From this side of history, I can count Naomi's blessings. She had a community to go back to, strength to pack up her things and to travel all the way back to that community. Her home was still there. She had been gone for over ten years and her home was still there and inhabitable. Who took care of it expecting her return? Just before this statement her pagan daughter-in-law had just declared such a love for her mother-in-law that could be envied by Cupid himself. Yet Naomi felt like she had nothing, when actually she had everything—the love of God, and the love of dear ones. She was well loved by the people in her community and family. Everything she needed was right under her nose yet in bitterness she could not see it. Still God did not give up on her. He was gracious to her and had mercy on her affliction. He gave her a creative idea to save her and her daughter-in-law. He used her in his plan to save his people.

Sometimes the things we mourn are intangible. What we are really mourning is an ideal, a picture of perfection we imagined but was never promised to us by God. We just thought "it's supposed to be this way," but then it turns out another way. A hurtful way. A way totally opposite of what we could ever have conceived in our hearts. A diagnosis, we mourn the loss of our good health, or the idea of living a vibrant healthy life, a child with a handicap, divorce or finding yourself in an unhappy marriage, the loss of happily ever after. We must mourn the loss, but moreover we have to reach forward to what God has left us with as Naomi finally did.

Because his mercies are new every morning (Lam. 3:23). It's in those times the devil comes along to convince us that we are not supposed to suffer. He uses part of God's word to convince us that suffering is not supposed to be part of our life if we serve God. He tried to tempt Jesus this way. He essentially told him because he was the son of God he was not supposed to suffer, so he could just take matters into his own hands and jump off the temple to prove it. Well, Jesus didn't fall for it. Literally, he told the devil where he could go and by doing so, he passed the test.

People have watched me suffer and have felt sorry for me. Some, seeing injustices done to me have expressed sympathy for me and expressed the sorrow they feel for my situation. But now I do not feel sorry for myself in my suffering. I can say as David said: *"it is good that I have been afflicted"* (*Psalm 119:71*). But there was a time when I had become very bitter at life, like Naomi. I went through a season of bitterness. A root of bitterness had sprung up in my heart due to all the things I had suffered, and I had become angry with God. An intense anger that just couldn't be assuaged. I felt like God just had it out for me. Like the prophet Jeremiah in the book of Lamentations. But unlike him, I had lost hope that things would ever change. Yet I had such fear of God that I wouldn't open up to him about it. I didn't turn to him, I turned away, and my heart became darker and darker. I tried to fix it myself so I read a book by Dr. James Dobson *When God Doesn't Make Sense*. And it helped—for a while. I read where he explained that God had suffered too by giving his only son to die for us. That helped—for a while.

The darkness left for a season, until something else bad happened and the darkness came back more violently than before. So, I read the book again, but the bitterness was so great that when I read that part again, I shook my (little earthly) fist in God's face and blamed him. I blamed him for my pain and for the pain Jesus, his own son had to go through. I said, "you see, you even did it to your own son!" I railed at him through my bitterness, blaming him for all the suffering and pain that ever happened. I was angry! How dare him! But later I discovered that bringing my pain and anger to him was the right thing to do. Maybe not the right way, but it was right to bring my pain to him because he is the only one who could do anything about it. And like the prophet Isaiah said, it was his love that delivered me from the pit of destruction. I found out later that God was holding on to me when I couldn't hold on myself.

To become angry at God for Jesus death means you don't believe that Jesus is God. Jesus said, *"I and my father are one"* (*John 10:30*). If you believe that Jesus is God, then you see Jesus' death as an act of love by God. But if you try to separate them then you believe Jesus' death was an act of cruelty by God perpetrated upon his son. (How

I saw it at the time in my anger). But the Word was made flesh and dwelt amongst us, and we beheld his glory. Jesus was the Word. Therefore, God is a loving God for stepping down from heaven to dwell amongst us and for laying down his life. Who could be mad at that?

People see everything through the lens of their own biases. We even read the Scriptures through the lens of our own biases. Sometimes when I am reading the Bible and I read about the slavery that was so common, I struggle with my feelings about injustice due to the fact my ancestors were slaves and great injustices were perpetrated on them. We focus on the fact of slavery but totally skip over the fact he's the one who miraculously sets slaves free. This is the pattern God shows us of his character. The devil creates havoc and God sets it right when we cry out to him. *"The righteous cry, and the Lord heareth, and delivereth them out of all their troubles" (Psalm 34:17)*. To truly get understanding we must willingly lay down our own biases and just let God speak to us through his Word. We have to trust in him with all of our heart. Even that part that was abused and still needs healing.

Through affliction I have gained so much more than what I lost. When we turn *to* God in our affliction, bringing our sorrow, pain, and brokenness to him, and not away from God, we are not cheated by life's sorrows, instead we gain. No one gets cheated who loves God and is called according to his purpose. His purpose makes all the difference. The scripture says: *"draw nigh to God and he will draw nigh to you" (James 4:8)*. The best time to draw nigh to God is when you're in the furnace of affliction. The Hebrew boys knew this. They didn't become bitter in affliction and persecution, but they turned to the Lord who was present with them in the fiery furnace. He brought them *through* the fire.

Your attitude towards God and your problems is very important. God gave us free-will because he wants to be chosen. He wants us to choose him. We must choose him every day and in every situation, no matter what. David (the man after God's heart) chose God over and over in affliction. David said: *"I will bless the Lord at all times: his praise shall continually be in my mouth" (Psalm 34:1)*. This Psalm was written when David was in trouble. Yet he didn't get angry and bitter against God; instead he worshipped. When David was depressed he commanded his soul to bless the Lord. He remembered the benefits of God and reminded his soul of God's righteousness (Psalm 103). What do you do when you face affliction?

When we draw nigh to God in our affliction, we learn so much about ourselves and about our God. We can see him as he is. We get to know "I Am". We get transported all the way back to the back side of the mountain to hear God say: *"I Am that I Am" (Exodus 3:14)*. And He Is. He is everything you need him to be. He is *Emanuel* the *dwell amongst us* God. He's in the affliction with us, walking with us, talking with us, being a fence all around us and bringing us through the fire. We learn who we are and where we stand in position to him. We learn about his love for us and even for those who have hurt us. We become more compassionate, tender hearted, merciful, and kind. Basically, we become more like him. He becomes our portion.

I always had a difficult time understanding the scriptures on God being our portion. But in the furnace of affliction when God is all you have, you understand that when all you need is him; you have the greatest portion. Our western minds have difficulty comprehending the Eastern culture. Thus, the concept of God being our portion, escapes our frame of reference. But you get a new perspective after going through the furnace of affliction and coming out with only God. When our lot in life seems to be only pain, anguish, and suffering and all we have to hold onto is the word of God, then the understanding of God as my portion becomes clear. Because when you have God, when you have turned to him and you are hiding in his bosom, everything else seems to fade away. He becomes everything you need. He becomes enough. You'll call him "I Am", and nothing can separate you from his love. It's only you and him. Your lot in life is to be his, and you are satisfied with that. If you suffer loss, he is able to restore. If you are broken down, he is able to rebuild you. If you have God, you have everything. You never have to fear the darkness.

Treasures in Darkness

"The earth was formless and empty, and darkness covered the deep waters. And the Spirit of God was hovering over the surface of the waters. Then God said, "Let there be light," and there was light. And God saw that the light was good. Then he separated the light from the darkness. God called the light "day" and the darkness "night." And evening passed and morning came, marking the first day."
Genesis 1:2-5, NLT

From the beginning God was above darkness. He has always had complete dominion over it. God named light and dark and then he pulled light out of darkness. When you have the power to name something, it means you own it. No one goes around naming things that don't belong to them (no rational person that is). Even though he called light good, he did not discard darkness. Anything that has a name can be subdued and conquered because the name of Jesus is higher than any name.

Next, God moved upon the darkness and touched it just as it was. The darkness didn't have to change itself to light and the void didn't have to fix itself before God fixed it. God meets us where we're at. We are not responsible for changing our darkness to light. What we are responsible for is bringing it to the one who is able to change it. Ephesians 5:11, tells us that we should expose darkness. We can have complete confidence in bringing it to God because he rules over darkness.

Sometimes life can get so dark that we cannot even see Jesus, but as Jesus told Thomas: *"Thomas, because thou hast seen me, thou hast believed: blessed are they that have not seen, and yet have believed" (John 20:29).* So often it seems like evil will prevail, but it never can. *"The light shines in the darkness, and the darkness can never extinguish it" (John 1:5, NLT).* Because the first thing God did in creation was separate light from darkness. God is so meticulous that he knows the dividing point between light and darkness. He is the only one that can tell us where light ends and darkness begins. One definition of light is happiness, and of darkness is adversity. These opposite emotions were mixed together and were part of the chaos. God took the time to separate the two from each other. It was a process. So much of a process that this is all he did on the first day. This explains why people feel so terrible when they experience mixed emotions. And why therapy brings relief. Separating the emotions sets the emotions back in their place. But it is a process to do so. God is still in control and always has the final say. This is where waiting comes in. If you can wait on the Lord, you will win. Believe that you are the light of the world and that no darkness can put your light out.

Darkness can be terrifying. Micah said, *"when I sit in darkness, the Lord will be a light unto me" (Micah 7:8)*. And the Hebrew children sang this Psalm: *"Woe is me, that I sojourn in Mesech, that I dwell in the tents of Kedar"(Psalm 120:5)*. This Psalm says that when I visit the violent (Meshech) it causes me to live in darkness (Kedar).

Yes, we may have to sit in darkness sometimes, but we are not alone, and we will not stay there. I remember a time when we had an infestation of mice in our house. We set out the little sticky traps to catch them in every place we observed them running. I had put one up against the baseboard of my bedroom wall, and one night I caught one. I woke up to the sound of the mouse trying to free itself from the sticky paper. But because it was dark I didn't know it was caught on the trap, and I sat up all night terrified that this noisy mouse in my room would get on my bed and bite me if I didn't stay diligent (don't judge me). So, I sat there, in the middle of my bed fear gripping my heart all throughout the night, until the dawn came. Finally, the light shined on the corner of the room where the mouse was caught. And then I saw, it was a little baby mouse caught on the sticky paper and the noise was him trying to get free. Talk about mixed feelings. The relief I felt at catching one of my tormentors was overshadowed only by the shame and regret I felt. I felt shame at being up all night afraid of a little baby mouse stuck to a piece of paper. I felt regret at losing a full night's sleep over harm that wasn't even possible. But darkness will do that to you. Scary things always seem ten times scarier at night, when it's dark. Darkness can bring about a paralyzing fear. For all of you judging me for not getting up and turning on the light, or just reaching for my phone and using the flashlight, hindsight is 20/20. Darkness can make it very hard to think rationally. Facts seem to dissipate, and feelings begin to rule in darkness. But the fact that God created darkness overrules the darkness when you turn to him.

There are treasures in the darkness, and God will reveal them to you if you live in him. He will give you double blessing for your shame. The first blessing is that the problem is fixed. The second blessing is to come out with treasures of darkness and a faith that can withstand any storm and God becomes your portion. You come out with relationship. A relationship with God is worth more than all the riches this world can offer.

One of the treasures of darkness I have seen is that the darker it gets in your life, the stronger your faith grows. You learn how to wait upon the Lord. The more they take from you, the more God gives to you. You receive strength in your spirit that no one can take away. You begin to rise. Not only do you rise, but peace rises within you. This is the peace of God which passes all understanding. There were times I should have been so worried with all the arrows aimed at me. All the past due bills and upcoming bills that I didn't have any idea how I would pay them. The need for strength to get through this or that. But I found that I had so much peace. A knowing that when I really needed it the money would be there. When I needed it, the strength would be there. My God shall supply all my needs according to his riches in glory. I could still worry about all manner of situations, my children, the future, my health, but by turning to God when the darkness arrived, I have received his "treasures of darkness."

How do you turn to God? Make sure you're connected to a church body that is founded on the word of God. Find people in that church who are truly connected to God (they love God and his people). In addition to the fellowship and teaching of your church, turn to the word of God daily. There is so much information available to help us turn to God. There are ministries on YouTube, Instagram, Facebook and other platforms. Ask God to guide you daily in your search. He said we should ask him to give us our daily bread. Then once God has delivered us from darkness we are responsible for releasing others. He empowers us to do this by holding our hands and walking us through our personal darkness. As he sits with us we need to sit with others and not judge them but assist them in their walk towards the light and out of darkness.

When Darkness Invades in Spite Of

But sometimes suffering can cause our relationship to become marred and discouragement can set in. When discouragement sets in it can be so hard to send up a praise. Even though you know God is good, and sovereign, and almighty. But discouragement can bring on a depression that causes the head to hang down, tears to flow, and hands to become heavy. It all goes back to process. God states what we are after the process. He knows the end from the beginning. It's up to us to walk it out. We have to walk through the process to become what God says we can become and do what God says we can do. It takes practice. Lots of practice of reading the word concerning our situation and practicing that word until we find ourselves walking in the light of what God told us. I learned this by walking through depression. I wrote the following poem as an ode to that time:

DEPRESSION
By: Cynthia Gibson-Dyse

You come unbidden like a stealthy lover arriving in the darkness.

But you are the darkness.

You wrap yourself around my soul and hold me,

You cling to me as a faithful friend.

You sit beside me daily as I go through my tasks.

You wait patiently for me as I walk thru the fog of your presence.

Your presence is felt though I try to ignore you and even shake you off.

Ah depression!

When will you go away?

I have walked through some dark times of dealing with depression due to the misery of the things I was suffering. There were even times I was suicidal, *"But thanks be to God who giveth us the victory through our Lord Jesus Christ" (1 Cor. 15:57)*. After my mother died, I thought I was okay. But I experienced a depression so tangible it sent me to therapy.

Nehemiah experienced a sadness like this when he heard about the destruction of Jerusalem. The place he called home that he loved so dearly but was taken captive from and brought to Babylon. Yet he held onto hope for his city. He tried to hide his sadness from the king, as many people suffering from depression do. You will smile in the daytime and cry at night. Holding yourself because there is no one around to hold you and comfort you in your despair. His response to the king when the king noticed his sad countenance was: *why should not my countenance be sad, when the city, the place of my fathers' sepulchres, lieth waste, and the gates thereof are consumed with fire (Neh. 2:3b)?*

Sadness is a proper response when terrible tragedies happen in our life. You do not have to feel guilty for feeling sad about a sad situation. The problem comes when the sadness lingers, and we can't find our way back to joy. We don't have to feel guilty about feeling sad. Guilt only adds to the problem. The Buddhists have a philosophy about suffering that says there are two arrows to suffering. The first arrow is the actual event that brings pain into our lives. We have no choice in the pain this arrow brings. Something painful happens to us and we feel that pain in our emotions. The second arrow we can choose to have or not. The second arrow is our reaction to the pain caused by the first arrow. The second arrow usually comes when we add "should" or "shouldn't" into the equation. "This shouldn't have happened to me," "I shouldn't feel this way." "They should have been more considerate of my feelings." "They should have protected me." What are we telling ourselves about the painful event that happened? Sometimes the second arrow hits its mark so deep that we need to go to a therapist to get it out. In order to change the way we feel, we must reconceptualize the story we are telling, or have told ourself about the painful event. And we may even need to learn new ways to express our feelings about the event.

Sadness is a feeling. Feelings were made to be felt and expressed. One of best things you can do for yourself when you are feeling sad, or any negative emotion, is to express those feelings and wait. Wait for God to turn it. *"Thou hast turned for me my mourning into dancing: thou hast put off my sackcloth, and girded me with gladness" (Psalm 30:11).* As a young mother I went through a period of deep sadness when my ex-husband, in an attempt to control me took my children from me and gave custody to his sister in Alabama. I was in the military, stationed stateside, and I would cry myself to sleep every night and talk to my "friends" about the situation. How I loved my children, how much I missed them, how unfair it was that he did this to me, and about my despair at ever getting custody of them again. I was expressing those sad feelings daily. But what I didn't know was that my "friends" were tired of hearing my story.

One day I happened to come upon some of my "friends" talking about me, saying things like, "she's always talking about her children." "She's always crying about her children." I was so mortified that my "friends" felt that way about me and voiced such judgements about me that I decided I would stop talking about it and crying about it. And I did. I just lived army life and "sucked it up" as they said in the army. But what I didn't know was that those emotions were still there, needing to be expressed. They were inside my body wreaking havoc with my immune system, and I discovered when I went to my new duty station that I was becoming bald in parts of my scalp. It's called Alopecia Areata, an autoimmune disease often brought on by severe stress. I went to a hairdresser in my new duty station, and she tried all sorts of treatments for my hair, but to no avail. Inside I knew what was happening. I made an appointment with the company chaplain and I told him my story. I cried and cried and cried (I think I used up a whole box of tissue in his office), and he let me. After that I decided I would continue to cry whenever I needed to and I would choose only certain people to talk to and express my feelings to until God turned it. And God did. Jeremiah prophesied that *"The young women will dance for joy, and the men-old and young-will join in the celebration. I will turn their mourning into joy. I will comfort them and exchange their sorrow for rejoicing" (Jeremiah 31:13, NLT).*

God is able to comfort us in ways we could never imagine, and we will rejoice just as Jeremiah prophesied. I did eventually regain custody of my children and I still rejoice. Remembering the pain of my suffering makes my times of rejoicing that much sweeter. If we have the ability to feel sadness, then we also have the capacity for joy, happiness, peace, gladness, all the positive emotions. And we can appreciate gladness because of our sad times.

"O my God, my soul is cast down within me: therefore will I remember thee from the land of Jordan, (the lowest places) *and of the Hermonites,* (the highest places) *from the hill Mizar" (Psalm 42:6).*

From the lowest lows of life to the highest highs, remembering who we belong to will keep us centered. The "land of Jordan" is a low part of the land of Israel where the river Jordan runs into the Dead Sea. The writer of this Psalm uses this as a euphemism for the low feelings of depression and the lowest times of his life. The "land of the Hermonites" was a mind picture of the three peaks of Mount Hermon, which represent the good times, times when the writer felt good and high on life. We have to remember God in our good times too. The writer of this Psalm directed his soul to remember God no matter the situation, in spite of the feelings that may have been tormenting him. The festivals and feasts God ordained when he brought his people out of captivity were set up for his people to remember. Remember that they had a God. Remember God's goodness to them. Remember to worship him. God wants us to remember him so that when we suffer our hearts will not fail, but we will be courageous and rise up whenever the enemy tries to knock us down.

"But the hour cometh, and now is, when the true worshippers shall worship the Father in spirit and in truth: for the Father seeketh such to worship him" (John 4:23).

Are you a true worshipper or a faker? Do you only "worship" God when things go your way? Is there a part of your heart you have reserved for yourself? A part you refuse to yield to him? So that when things don't go the way you planned, or the way you want you can snatch it back from him, and shake your fist and say, "see, I trusted you but now look!" True worshippers worship *in spite of*. The AMPC version of this verse defines the word truth as *in reality*. True worship is worshipping God in your reality, as opposed to the way you want it to be.

When your emotions begin to torment you, you can talk to your heart, the seat of your emotions, and remind yourself of who your God is, and how he is for you, not against you. Trust in God. Trust is a choice. This is where your free-will is activated. Free-will is our gift from God. This is the part that is in our control, choosing to trust or not. One way to do this is to remember past victories that only he could have given you. He has done great things in your life before but it's so easy to forget. This is what it means to "let not your heart be troubled, neither let it be afraid." You control it by remembering the goodness and the greatness and the reality of the love of God for you. Don't even let your mind go there, but if it does, don't let it stay there. Then God, even our own God (our personal God) will (help) bless us (Psalm 67:6, my paraphrase).

Our Attitude in Suffering

"If it be so, our God whom we serve is able to deliver us from the burning fiery furnace, and he will deliver us out of thine hand, O king. But if not, be it known unto thee, O king, that we will not serve thy gods, nor worship the golden image which thou hast set up"
Daniel 3:17-18

An attitude is the external expression of an internal feeling. The Hebrew boys had attitude with "O king." They were "reading" him like "you can sit up there on that throne and pass judgement on us if you want to. But let me tell you something "O king", the God I serve is more powerful than even you and is able to deliver me, but if not, I will not serve any other God. Mister!" Their attitude with this king was one of obstinate indignation. Justifiably so. They had a trust in their God that could not be shaken.

Mary and Joseph experienced homelessness for a short time. In movies the birth of Jesus is depicted as happening as soon as they arrive in Bethlehem. But we see by the Scriptures that they were living there for a while before she gave birth. They had to live in this stable, homeless until after the birth of Jesus. The parents and the infant Messiah were homeless. Yet when things don't go our way, when we don't get to live as richly as we would like, what is our attitude? I have never read about Mary fussing at Joseph about their living conditions. *"First you didn't believe me, now you got me living like some kind of animal…"* And the Bible is very transparent concerning thoughts and attitudes of the characters.

God is a God that goes with us through the fire. David said, *"yeah though I walk through the valley of the shadow of death…" (Psalm 23)*, and God told Isaiah, "When you walk through the fire you will not be burnt or even scorched" (Isaiah 43:2). I don't know about you, but any mortal who walks through fire will get burned. You cannot walk through a fire without some kind of protection on and not get burned or scorched. Only God can allow us to walk through fire. He did it before. For defying him "O King" had the three Hebrew boys thrown into the fiery furnace. Later the king looked in and they were walking around in the fire. Just taking a stroll with Jesus. They must have been walking around for quite some time too, because the heat from the furnace killed the soldiers who threw them in. Yet, when the king came close, he was not harmed. This tells me that the furnace had cooled down significantly. God will walk with us for as long as it takes. He said he will never leave us nor forsake us (Hebrews 13:5). And He won't.

We don't always suffer because we did something wrong. Sometimes we suffer because we are doing right. In Psalm 44:22 we read, *"… for your sake (God) we are killed all the day long."* God's chosen people were suffering terribly at the hands of their enemies, even though they were doing right. The writer was so confused. When you do right, isn't right supposed to happen? When you do good, aren't good things supposed to come back to you? Aren't good things supposed to happen to good people and bad things to bad people? It's only right, isn't it? Yet in this Psalm and in Lamentations the third chapter, we see good people suffering. This is where the devil fights us the most. Making us feel justified in our anger with God. Projecting his anger with God on us. Using us as his vessel to retaliate on God for casting him down for his wickedness. Don't let yourself be used as a tool by the devil. Turn his weapon on him and turn TO God in worship when you begin to feel angry because of your painful circumstances. Though they may be unjust, if you will endure and worship, you will come out victorious. God does have a good plan for your life. One day, he will use it all to his glory. We can never forget that our enemy is lurking out there. He hates us, and is out to destroy our faith in God. He does not want us to turn to God and have relationship with him. Remember Job, Elisabeth and Zacharias, Mary and Joseph? Attitude is everything and our attitude is the only thing we have control over. Consequently, we need to make sure to keep our attitude right.

Caleb followed God wholly and yet suffered an extra 45 years due to the unbelief of his community.

> And Moses sware on that day, saying, Surely the land whereon thy feet have trodden shall be thine inheritance, and thy children's for ever, because thou hast wholly followed the Lord my God. And now, behold, the Lord hath kept me alive, as he said, these forty and five years, even since the Lord spake this word unto Moses, while the children of Israel wandered in the wilderness: and now, lo, I am this day fourscore and five years old. Joshua 14:9-10

Sometimes our community can drag us down, but if we will stay faithful to God and follow him wholly he will bring us out and our righteousness will shine as the light of day. Micah said: *"Rejoice not against me, O mine enemy: when I fall, I shall arise; when I sit in darkness, the Lord shall be a light unto me" (Micah 7:8)*. And what a great light he is. He is the light that will help me rise. The true light that shines into my darkness and lifts me. But the writer said "when" I fall, and "when" I sit in darkness. Saying the word "when" implies that the writer knows for sure these things are going to happen. He was a prophet, of course he knew, but he also had assurance that when the bad things happened God would be right there. And that is the very same assurance we have. Bad things will happen, but be assured that when they do you have a savior to whom you can turn and he will be a light unto you. And he will bring you out.

There is no *testimony* without a *test*. And God allows us to have tests to have a testimony. And we have a testimony to defeat the enemy. Therefore, as Peter said:

> Beloved, think it not strange concerning the fiery trial which is to try you, as though some strange thing happened unto you: But rejoice, inasmuch as ye are partakers of Christ's sufferings; that, when his glory shall be revealed, ye may be glad also with exceeding joy.
> 1 Peter 4:12-13

> For his anger lasts only a moment, but his favor lasts a lifetime; weeping may stay for the night, but rejoicing comes in the morning. Psalm 30:5, NIV

Suffering is temporary. Morning always comes after night.

God Remembers

> *"O LORD, how long will you forget me? Forever? How long will you look the other way? How long must I struggle with anguish in my soul, with sorrow in my heart every day? How long will my enemy have the upper hand?*
> *Psalm 13:1-2, NLT*

I cannot tell you how many times I have prayed this same prayer as David. Not only have I prayed it, but I have also tried to do the math myself to figure out how long I was going to have to suffer. I studied the lives of David, Joseph, Jeremiah, and Job. Habakkuk, Naomi, Jesus, Mary and Joseph. I tried to add up the years, (carry the one) and divide by I don't know what. But I have never been able to decipher or cipher just how long a certain trial was going to last. It ends when it ends, and only God Most High knows when that will be.

With God, timing is crucial. The Bible often talks about the "acceptable time." When his children were suffering in Babylonian captivity, God sent the prophets to encourage them. In the book of Isaiah, the 49th chapter and the 8th verse, God told them *"When the time comes to save you, I will show you favor and answer your cries for help."* The King James version translates that as "acceptable time." Just know that in your time of suffering God does not forget, he does see, and he does care.

God's answer: *"Can a mother forget the baby at her breast and have no compassion on the child she has borne? Though she may forget, I will not forget you! (Isa. 49:15, NIV)*. The Lord will not forget you. But these scriptures by implication tell you the wait will be long, so long that you will think he has forgotten you, but verse 23 says *"they shall not be ashamed that wait for me."*

The Bible gives us some examples of people that did not wait on God and the dire consequences they faced afterwards. Saul could not wait for Samuel to come and give the sacrifice. Sarai could not wait for God to open her womb. And they both deeply regretted not waiting. The eleven disciples didn't wait on God after Judas left their number. *"So now we must choose a replacement for Judas from among the men who were with us the entire time we were traveling with the Lord Jesus-from the time he was baptized by John until the day he was taken from us. Whoever is chosen will join us as a witness of Jesus' resurrection"* *(Acts 1:21-22 NLT)*. The disciples knew the scriptures. They understood that it was necessary to replace Judas. But what they didn't understand was God's way of choosing and his timing. God intended for Saul (who became Paul) to take Judas' place as a witness and 12th apostle; but the disciples felt the urgent need to fill that spot, so they did it the only way they knew how. They forgot God's ways are higher than ours and his thoughts are not even like ours. His timing is perfect, and he will act to fulfill all his promises and his word will come to pass. Have you ever become impatient with God?

To wait is to look for, hope, or expect. It takes strength and courage to wait but, *"Be strong and let your heart take courage, all you who wait for and hope for and expect the Lord!" (Psalm 31:24, AMPC)*. While we wait, we can experience a lot of strong emotions. The anxiety level alone that waiting causes…. So not only do we need to take courage, but we also need to take back all of our emotions with God's help. Here is an example of taking back your emotions: I used to lose a lot of joyful things when I had a relationship breakup. I couldn't enjoy the places we used to go that brought me pleasure, or the scents I enjoyed wearing when we were together because they reminded me of the relationship and brought sadness. But one day I decided not to let anyone steal my joy from me again. I took back my emotions. I decided to continue enjoying the places I loved, and I decided to wear the scents I loved, and guess what? They continued to bring me joy. All I lost was a relationship that was bad for me. So, after mourning my loss I moved on and kept my peace and *Joii de vie*. We have power over our emotions. They don't have power over us. While we wait, we can steady ourselves and still our hearts and ask God to soothe our doubts and calm our fears until he remembers us. *"For the vision is yet for an appointed time, but at the end it shall speak, and not lie: though it tarry, wait for it; because it will surely come, it will not tarry" (Habakkuk 2:3)*. An "appointed time" is an acceptable time. Everything that God said happened because he said it. The Bible doesn't say how long it took to happen. It just tells us that it happened. When God was creating the world he just said it, and it happened, and it was so. If God says it's going to happen, it will. No matter how long it takes. Always hold on to his word. He *will* remember you.

"…God remembered Noah" (Gen. 8:1). "…God remembered Abraham" (Gen. 19:29). "…God remembered Rachel" (Gen. 30:22). "…God remembered his covenant with Abraham, with Isaac, and with Jacob" (Ex. 2:24). "He hath remembered his mercy and his truth toward the house of Israel…" (Ps. 98:3). And God remembered the iniquity of Babylon to punish her. And God promised to remember his children when they went to war and were being oppressed by their enemies if they would sound the alarm as he had instructed them. And he will remember us if we will sound our alarm when we are being oppressed by all manner of evil. Our alarm is prayer, praise, worship, and turning to our God.

Chapter Eight

Hope Deferred

Proverbs 13:12 says: *"Hope deferred makes the heart sick."* (How sick do you have to be to try to calculate God's timing?) It's painful and agonizing to hope when the thing you have hoped for takes too long to come. You don't want to hope because dashed hope is more painful to you than not having it. It can twist up your insides. It can change the way you view the world. The Bible illustrates this through the lives of various people who had given up hope in their situation changing. We get to view firsthand how it changed them and ultimately how God's miracle working power through suffering changed their lives and brought greatness to their doorsteps.

There was a childless Shunamite woman who encountered the Prophet Elijah. And for her kindness towards him Elijah told her: *"Next year at this time you will be holding a son in your arms!"* Her reply was, *"No, my lord!" she cried. "O man of God, don't deceive me and get my hopes up like that" (2 Kings 4:16, NLT)*. I believe that she did not say this in a monotone voice. The Bible says she cried or screamed this out. Because she had already settled that longtime longing of her heart and did not want it to be disturbed. She had taken her dreams and wrapped them in Egyptian cotton and tissue paper and stashed them behind her heart and guarded them with the fierceness of a mother bear protecting her cubs. She never wanted to feel the pain of unfulfilled desire again. She knew that once you have settled your heart, stirring up the longings again can cause a pain that shatters your inward parts so that there is no power on earth that can restore them. She understood the proverb: *"...by sorrow of the heart the spirit is broken" (15:13)*. Or as The New Living Translation declares, *"a broken heart crushes the spirit"*. Have you ever had a sorrowful heart? Have you ever had to *stash* your dreams so no one would be able to *dash* your dreams?

Suffering can make you lose your trust in God. Especially when it lasts a long time. When though you believe IN him, you may stop believing him because you don't want to get your hopes up, only to be dashed to the ground again. You won't let your heart believe, even if an angel came to you because it hurts too much.

> There was in the days of Herod, the king of Judaea, a certain priest named Zacharias, of the course of Abia: and his wife was of the daughters of Aaron, and her name was Elisabeth. And they were both righteous before God, walking in all the commandments and ordinances of the Lord blameless. And it came to pass, that while he executed the priest's office before God in the order of his course, there appeared unto him an angel of the Lord standing on the right side of the altar of incense. Luke 1:5, 6, 11

Righteous, blameless, God fearing, people often suffer (See Job 1:1). But God always has a plan for greater. They were minding their own business. And doing God's business, faithfully, yet they suffered. A long time. *And they had no child, because that Elisabeth was barren, and they both were now well stricken in years (Luke 1:7)*. Zacharias and Elizabeth suffered a long time because to be childless in those days was a disgrace in the eyes of society. So, they suffered from shame struggling with it for a long time before accepting it as their lot. But they stayed faithful in serving God. They had to suffer the pain of dashed hope. As a priest in the temple it's possible that Zacharias was called on to read the Scriptures on Sabbath. What went through his mind when he read how God gave a child to Sarah and Abraham, Isaac and Rebecca, Manoah and his wife, Elkanah and Hannah? How long did he hope before it became too painful to read those scriptures? Yet he served. Faithfully. How many evil neighbors did he see conceive children and treat their children poorly? What questions rolled through his mind at night before dozing off to sleep? How many nights did he have to hold Elizabeth as she cried herself to sleep because she had no child? Where did they bury the pain? Just as years later Mary and Martha buried their brother Lazarus as they gave up hope that Jesus would arrive in time to heal him.

Zacharias believed in God, he was a priest, and yet the dichotomy of faith for something to happen in the future and the reality of now can take your life into a tailspin. When you want to believe that the good thing is going to happen, yet all you can see in front of you is the bad, grappling with this is what causes many to get frustrated and turn back. This is what was happening to the children of Israel in the wilderness. Because the promise seemed so far away, and all they could see was wilderness, pain, and suffering, they wanted to throw in the towel and go back to Egypt.

But the angel said to him, "Do not be afraid, Zacharias, because your petition [in prayer] was heard, and your wife Elizabeth will bear you a son, and you will name him John (Luke 1:13, AMP). "Your petition was heard" tells me he had been praying this prayer before. Probably for as long as his wife was of childbearing age. Now both of them were too old naturally. Can't God make you wait? Elizabeth's period comes month after month. How many months of waiting in those years? The questions: why Lord why? When Lord when? Do you care? Do you see? Doing right but wrong keeps happening. Where we see pain (shame, unfulfilled desires, longing, fear of the future...) God sees purpose. John would be raised differently by older parents than he would if his parents were young, full of life and their own ideas. *All this happened in order to fulfill what the Lord had spoken through the prophet [Isaiah]: (Matthew 1:22, AMP).* This prophecy was a long time coming. Isaiah was long dead. Yet God fulfilled his prophecy. They were old when their blessing finally came. They survived. Not only did they survive, but they survived until God made them to see gladness: *"And thou shalt have joy and gladness; and many shall rejoice at his birth"* (Luke 1:14). And not only them, but Anna the prophetess:

> And there was one Anna, a prophetess, the daughter of Phanuel, of the tribe of Aser: she was of a great age, and had lived with an husband seven years from her virginity; And she was a widow of about fourscore and four years, which departed not from the temple, but served God with fastings and prayers night and day. And she coming in that instant gave thanks likewise unto the Lord, and spake of him to all them that looked for redemption in Jerusalem. Luke 2:36

Even if you've suffered for years God knows how to bring you joy and gladness. Anna waited a long time to see the promise of God over her life, and through faithfulness it was fulfilled.

"And Zacharias said unto the angel, Whereby shall I know this? for I am an old man, and my wife well stricken in years," (Luke 1:18). You can question God and still serve him. This question has attitude with it. Like Mary and Martha asking Jesus "where were you? My brother wouldn't have died if you had been here to heal him! Haven't we been faithful?" "When you came to our home bringing 12 extra guests, didn't we serve you, and them? Didn't we walk together and talk together and eat and play together?" "Where were you Jesus, Huh?" "Where were you!" The Bible does say we have no right to argue with our maker (Isaiah 45:9). But we can ask him questions. Habakkuk, Mary, Job, for example.

You may even have to take your questions to therapy, because *Hope deferred makes the heart sick" (Proverbs 13:12, NIV).* Or as *The Message* says: *"Unrelenting disappointment leaves you heartsick."* When you have a broken leg, you can't run a race. When you are sick, you become physically weak and can't do many of the things you were formerly able to do. Consequently, when your spirit is broken, running life's race becomes very difficult if not impossible without help. And when your heart is sick it's very difficult to do the things that formerly brought you happiness. This is called "anhedonia," the inability to feel pleasure. It's a symptom of depression, or, a sick heart. The Bible says that the woman who had the spirit of infirmity for eighteen years could in no wise lift herself up. For eighteen years she walked around with this infirmity, and no one was able to help her get well, and she couldn't help herself.

This woman is a great picture of God's people. In the Bible, before Jesus's birth his people were longing for Messiah to deliver them. They were so oppressed by the Roman government and could in no wise lift themselves up out of this oppression. Many men had emerged and tried to be the deliverer, but these men failed miserably and were captured by the Roman government and executed, effectively ending their deliverance. This left God's people feeling helpless and hopeless.

Helplessness can bring on hopelessness. When you become hopeless it's hard to think rationally. It seems like the world is so dark and your problems are so big. In these times it's important to hold on to the promises of God. Just be sure they are from him and not just something you conjured up in your imagination. That will only lead to bitterness, disappointment, cynicism and sometimes a deep emotional hole you cannot dig your way out of. Your heart may be sick right now because hope has been deferred, but he is "Jehovah Rapha" the God that heals. He's a high priest that can be touched by our infirmities (Hebrews 4:15). But even when our heart is sick and our spirit is so broken that we can in no wise lift ourselves, there is always something left that we *can* do. Even though she couldn't raise herself up, she knew where to go. She didn't sit around complaining about not being able to raise herself up, instead she went to church. She did what she *could* do. The scripture says Jesus was in the synagogue when he saw her.

God will always leave us with a remnant. A remnant of strength. A remnant of health. A remnant of self-esteem. A remnant of people who still believe in us and love us. When Jacob wrestled with the angel and the angel disjointed his thigh, Jacob did not lay down and quit. Jacob said, "I'm not going to let go until you bless me." He had a remnant of strength, intestinal fortitude. He kept doing whatever he was able to do. It wasn't enough to defeat the angel, but he held on until time shifted and the angel blessed him for his tenacity. If you can't do anything, hold on. While you're holding on do whatever you can that is right. If you're so depressed you can't even get out of bed, lay there and say, "Lord I bless you." "You are good, and your mercy endures forever!" "There is no God like you!"

The best thing you can do is carry your sick heart and broken spirit to the throne of his grace. For we have an high priest that understands, sympathizes and has compassion on our weaknesses and infirmities. We can take our brokenness to his feet as a child brings his broken toy to his father, and have the faith of that child that our father is willing and able to fix it and make everything alright. I've seen children bring toys that were irrevocably broken to their father's feet and ask them to fix it. And while I knew (and that parent knew) there was absolutely nothing that could be done to fix that toy; the faith of that child in its parent was expressed by the act of bringing it to his father. *"For the Son of man is come to seek and to save that which was lost" (Luke 19:10).* The word *lost* in this context means *broken beyond repair* or *destroyed.* The same Greek word is used for destroy in this next scripture: *"The thief cometh not, but for to steal, and to kill, and to destroy: I am come that they might have life, and that they might have it more abundantly" (John 10:10).* Our father is not like an earthly father. Our father is God all by himself and is everything we need him to be. He is able to do exceedingly and abundantly above all that we can ask or think. Our father is good and wants us to be whole, and wants us to bring our brokenness to him so that he can fix it. The only thing needed on our part is faith in him.

There is currently a movement in the therapeutic community towards mindfulness. Although I do believe in being mindful, and I do believe in meditation, specifically meditating on the word of God (the Bible specifically says we should), I believe there is a time and a season for everything. It's okay to buck the current trend and set your sights on something unseen. Sometimes when we are suffering and our mind is sick it is almost impossible to remain present enough to meditate. In those times, when our heart is sick, we need to lean into faith. For *"faith is the substance of things hoped for and the evidence of things not seen (Hebrews 11:1)."* Does that sound like being present to you? I don't think so. Paul said, *"I focus on this one thing: forgetting the past and looking forward to what lies ahead" (Philippians 3:13, NLT).* This is hope. Faith and hope work together to heal the sick at heart.

Depression (or a sick heart) comes when we lose hope, but faith and hope walk us hand in hand into the promises of God. *"[With eyes of] faith Isaac, looking far into the future, invoked blessings upon Jacob and Esau" (Gen. 27:27-29, 39-40, Hebrews 11:20, AMPC).* Depression can feel like being paralyzed. *"And a certain man lame from his mother's womb was carried, whom they laid daily at the gate of the temple which is called Beautiful, to ask alms of them that entered into the temple" (Acts 3:2).* This man sat at the gate daily watching everyone else living their lives; going home, traveling, being in love, having children, playing, laughing, and worshipping inside the temple. All the things he was unable to do because he was paralyzed. As a result, his physical infirmity led to an emotional ailment. He sat at the gate daily to do his everyday thing, surviving. He sat there hoping only in the goodness or dutifulness of others so that he could get by. If he could just collect enough money from enough people looking on him and feeling sorry for him (and secretly glad it wasn't them) then he could survive one more day to come back and do it again. His very existence was glum. But one day he was fortunate enough to be at the right place at the right time to meet the right people. People who knew about and carried the power of the one true and living God inside them. And this man, obeying their words, received a miracle.

I can give you example after example of people who held on to faith and hope to get through the current trouble they were facing. As a matter of fact, the eleventh chapter of Hebrews does it for me. It ends telling us about the people who never even received relief from their suffering on this earth, but held on to their faith and received "divine approval" instead. So, wrap up your sick heart and take it to the foot of the cross, and let the healing blood of Jesus drip onto it and you will rise up in healing. As the writer of Hebrews tells us, *"Let us therefore come boldly unto the throne of grace, that we may obtain mercy, and find grace to help in time of need" (Heb. 4:16).*

When All Hope Seems Lost

> *"The other disciples therefore said unto him, We have seen the Lord. But he said unto them, Except I shall see in his hands the print of the nails, and put my finger into the print of the nails, and thrust my hand into his side, I will not believe."*
> John 20:25

Thomas had lost hope. He had believed Jesus was the Messiah and his hopes were cruelly crushed. When hope has been crushed over and over, we can become like Thomas or Zacharias and doubt, or refuse to believe again. At one time, I too felt that way. I had gone through so much trauma and abuse that I gave up on hope of an expected end. I even went to the point of thinking maybe God isn't real. I became agnostic in my thinking. But God in his grace had so much mercy on me as to prove himself over and over again, until I could believe again. As with Thomas, he showed that his love and grace will cover even our unbelief. He is willing to, and will go to great lengths to prove to us that he is real, that he loves us, and that his word is true. And that is even more awesome being that our salvation is predicated on faith.

"Then the eleven disciples went away into Galilee, into a mountain where Jesus had appointed them. And when they saw him, they worshipped him: but some doubted" (Matthew 28:16-17). God loves us even when we doubt. We are still his. Just be honest with him about your doubt. Take it to him. Don't try to make yourself believe. He will teach you to trust. He did it for me. He is still the God that created something out of nothing. He can create faith where unbelief lies. We don't have to manufacture it, because he loves us, so he reaches down into the chaos of our heart and creates everything we need in it to be his child and to serve him. I call him awesome. God will provide the faith he requires us to have.

The heart may be sick now because you have waited a long time and your dream was deferred. But the end of Proverbs 13:12 in the King James Version says "when" the desire cometh. "When" is a sure word.

It means it's going to happen. So, when your heart gets sick, do what the doctors tell you. Rest, take your medicine, and stay hydrated. Rest in God and in his promises. Take the medicine of the Word. And drink of the fountain of life freely.

The Wait

"Wait on the Lord: be of good courage, and he shall strengthen thine heart: wait, I say, on the Lord." Psalms 27:14

The answer to a sick heart is waiting on the Lord. Not waiting as in do nothing, but a good wait would be going to therapy. Working through your issues that made your heart sick. When you are depressed, sometimes you just can't get up by yourself. You need help. You need help from a particular person or other people who care about you and can help you to get a new perspective. The greatest complement I have ever received from any of my clients is when they said: "Oh, I never thought of it that way." This tells me I have given them the gift of a new perspective. The Bible says that knowing the truth makes us free. Getting a new perspective is the first step towards knowing the truth about yourself, about God, about your situation, or about others. The truth will always be the truth and it will always be out there, but until you know it you will remain bound.

The Bible says it's the truth that you know that sets you free. And you can ask God to help you to know the truth about you so that you can be set free. Because God "so" (extremely) loves us that he wants us to know our truth and be set free. He's not sitting in heaven hiding it from us. He's just waiting for us to want to know and to get involved in our own process and ask him. This is relationship. And relationship with his creation is God's ultimate goal. Understanding how much we are loved by a holy God gives us a tiny glimpse into heaven. It helps us to be reconciled to our creator, and Paul said there is nothing that can separate us from that love (Romans 8:28). Imagine if you will that God's love is like rain and you are standing under an open heaven. As his love showers down on you it's healing you, restoring your soul, and setting you free from your past. His love is cleansing you, washing away anything that stands between you and him.

Second Corinthians 10:4 says, *"the weapons of our warfare are not carnal,"* and they are not, because our enemies are not carnal. But when we are fighting something natural, we need to fight with something natural. If someone broke into your home, you wouldn't stand around quoting scriptures at them. You would probably call the police, or if they attacked you, you might even grab a bat or a lamp or something to fight them off. We fight disease in our body with medicine. Isn't it prudent of us to fight for our mental health with every weapon available? God *so* (extremely) loved us that he gave...

- Us feelings like him
- The ability/language to define and express our emotions when they hurt or just to share them when we are glad
- That lump that gets in our throat when we need to express sadness
- Tears to wash that lump away
- People with the gift in them to listen compassionately

We have to fight for our mental health because it controls our spiritual health. Jude told us, "*Ye should earnestly contend for the faith which was once delivered unto the saints.* We must fight for our faith on every level (Jude 3).

Second Corinthians 10:4, also tells us that we need to bring our thoughts into captivity. Many people don't even know what that means and have difficulty managing their thoughts on their own. Consequently, spiritual depression can come when natural depression isn't resolved. As a Christian sealed by God you cannot be possessed by evil spirits, but they can oppress you. Which is basically bullying you with your own thoughts about you and what happened to you. It's mental pressure. When you come into agreement with those evil spirits you become oppressed. When we go into therapy or counseling and begin to talk about our issues in a confidential environment we expose the darkness within. You can't change what you don't admit.

The Bible wouldn't tell you to wait if a change wasn't going to come. To truly endure we have to have a "though he slay me yet will I trust him" faith. In order to accomplish this, he has to allow us to be in situations that we really think we're going to be slain. Like Jacob, though he breaks something significant in my life (as when Jacob wrestled with the angel and the angel broke his hip) I will still hold onto him. Like Jeremiah in the 3rd chapter of Lamentations, it was God that allowed all the pain. Yet Jeremiah believed in new mercies every morning and the great faithfulness of his God. When you have a "though he slay me" type of faith, you are essentially acknowledging God as the resurrection and the life. You have a deep faith in him as the creator of the universe. You're telling him that even if he slays you, you understand that he has the power to raise you back up.

The Children of Israel had to wait many times in captivity for the Lord to deliver them from the hands of their enemies. One such time the Lord actually warned them that they were going to be there a long time:

> Thus saith the Lord of hosts, the God of Israel, unto all that are carried away captives, whom I have caused to be carried away from Jerusalem unto Babylon; Build ye houses, and dwell in them; and plant gardens, and eat the fruit of them; Take ye wives, and beget sons and daughters; and take wives for your sons, and give your daughters to husbands, that they may bear sons and daughters; that ye may be increased there, and not diminished. And seek the peace of the city <u>whither I have caused you to be carried away captives,</u> and pray unto the Lord for it: for in the peace thereof shall ye have peace. For thus saith the Lord of hosts, the God of Israel; Let not your

prophets and your diviners, that be in the midst of you, deceive you, neither hearken to your dreams which ye cause to be dreamed. For they prophesy falsely unto you in my name: I have not sent them, saith the Lord. For thus saith the Lord, That after seventy years be accomplished at Babylon I will visit you, and perform my good word toward you, in causing you to return to this place. Jeremiah 29:4-10

God commanded them to get comfortable in their captivity because he sent it and was not going to deliver them until he was ready. Don't believe God is in control, that he is the one that allows pain and suffering? *"The <u>LORD</u> makes poor and makes rich; <u>He</u> brings low and <u>He</u> lifts up" (1 Samuel 2:7, AMP).*

Sometimes we lie to ourselves when we do not want to accept our suffering. Sometimes we think serving God means no problems or suffering. We tell ourselves that "God wants us to be happy" or "God wants the best for me" or other made-up drivel that is not in the Bible and get frustrated when we suffer. But this is a misconception. The problem here is that God's definition of his best and our definition of best are so different. Serving God means having a relationship with the One who holds all power and knows the end from the beginning. God's strength is made perfect (or complete) in our weakness. Things won't make us happy. However, having a right relationship with God will bring happiness.

The things I don't have can't make me sad, because when I think about all the blessings I do have I get joy. If we lack, then God gets to show his power. When we state "God wants what's best for me" we're quoting the world (or Baal). But when we stay with the word of God, *"His strength is made perfect in our weakness" "His grace (graciousness, favor) is sufficient" (2 Cor 12:9)* then we are confessing what God declares, (the truth) about our situation. Actually, there is more in the Bible about God's people suffering than people want to admit. The truth is this world is not our home. God didn't put us here or save us to be happy in it. That may have been his first plan, but human nature and sin brought about a change in plans. When sin came into this world (through Adam) suffering came with it. But along with suffering came God's plan for redemption, which also included suffering. Sometimes the way through suffering is *through* suffering. We have to walk through it and turn to God for strength. We must pray for our enemies and seek peace where we normally would not. Looking to God as the author and finisher of our faith to be with us in it and bring us out victorious in the end. Because if God is the finisher of our faith it means there is an end. Hold on through sickness, through pain, through lack, disappointment, whatever storm, whatever void, walk through it knowing the master of the wind is in control and will not suffer your foot to be moved.

Habakkuk waited, and in his waiting attained "though he slay me" type of faith. In answer to Habakkuk's question "How Long?" God said: *"This vision is for a future time. It describes the end, and it will be fulfilled. If it seems slow in coming, wait patiently, for it will surely take place. It will not be delayed" (Habakkuk 2:3, NLT).* This is a famous scripture about waiting on God to provide justice. It seems to contradict itself, but it doesn't. It really says, "if it takes a long time, wait for it anyway, because it will not be late." When suffering long, it can feel as if God is going to come too late. He waits until zero hour to act, and sometimes even then he is silent. As a result, we lose the house, the car, get evicted, divorced, and we just don't understand why. How could a God that is good and all powerful let this happen? He's still never too late. Because he is all powerful. He can restore the house, the car, the apartment, the marriage. He can even restore lost years. He told the prophet Joel this (Joel 2:25). The book of Habakkuk is a conversation between God and the prophet Habakkuk. To have conversation you need to have relationship. And when you have the right relationship you get to ask the hard questions. Conversations consist of asking questions and listening to the answers and then considering the answers. Mull them over in your mind. Then ask more questions if you need to. But listen with your heart when the answers come.

Because of God's answer to Habakkuk, he was able to profess this statement of complete faith: *"...I will wait quietly for the coming day when disaster will strike the people who invade us. Even though the fig trees have no blossoms, and there are no grapes on the vines; even though the olive crop fails, and the fields lie empty and barren; even though the flocks die in the fields, and the cattle barns are empty, yet I will rejoice in the Lord! I will be joyful in the God of my salvation!" (Habakkuk 3:16-18 NLT).* These were not just words to Habakkuk, he actually saw all of this and more come to pass before his eyes. In his lifetime. Is there a *yet* praise in you? When it seems like God is not listening. When it seems like he doesn't care, can you yet praise him? This is when he gets glory in front of his enemies, when we say "I don't care what's going on, I don't care what it looks like, you are my God, the air I breathe, the song I sing. I love you LORD. You are God all by yourself! You are the lifter of my head." This is how we make his praise glorious. If he allows us to suffer and we still turn to him in worship and praise, he looks great to his enemies. We make his praise glorious. Suffering is a part of the Christian experience. Longsuffering (fortitude, strength of mind that enables a person to bear pain or adversity) is a fruit of the spirit. We all suffer long in some area of our lives. Sometimes it is of an emotional, financial, or health nature. But when we know that our redeemer lives, somehow, it's okay. We know that it's going to work out for our good.

We live in peace until our appointed time. God is working on the left-hand where we can't see (Job 29:3). God wants us to need him and wait on him. He created us to make his praise glorious. All of our struggles have purpose. We are always concerned about how we look to others but God is concerned about how we look to his enemies because his ways are higher than our ways, his thoughts higher than our thoughts.

And at the end of Habakkuk's statement of faith he said: *"The Lord God is my strength, and he will make my feet like hinds' feet, and he will make me to walk upon mine high places…" (Habakkuk 3:19).* "High places" denote perspective. If you could just get up a little higher you could see things differently. God has high places. David recognized this. He wrote: *"He maketh my feet like hinds' feet, and setteth me upon my high places" (Psalms 18:33).* Not only will God take you high enough to gain perspective, but they will also be "your" high places. No one can beat you at being you. God has special places designed for just you. And when you get there you will be so confident that no one can shake you from that place. The struggle and our response to the struggle transports us to our high places.

"In your patience possess ye your souls," (Luke 21:19). This is the secret to winning in life—being patient in the process. Don't believe the lies: "this is not working" or "nothing's changing." The devil knows that if you endure the hard stuff, weather the storms, batten the hatches, endure the tedious, walk through the deserts, you will win. Your soul is the most important part of you. Your soul is your mind, will, and emotions. Having patience in trying times means to stand fast and hold on. Hold on to what? To your faith. To your relationship with God. To his Word. This will keep your soul intact no matter what life throws at you. Hebrews 3:6 tells us that we are Christ's house *"if we hold fast the confidence and the rejoicing of the hope firm unto the end."* So, Christ will dwell in, abide in, reside in us if we do this-hold our confidence and the rejoicing of the hope firm unto the end.

It's Never Too Late

> *And, behold, there cometh one of the rulers of the synagogue, Jairus by name; and when he saw him, he fell at his feet, and besought him greatly, saying, My little daughter lieth at the point of death: I pray thee, come and lay thy hands on her, that she may be healed; and she shall live. While he yet spake, there came from the ruler of the synagogue's house certain which said, Thy daughter is dead: why troublest thou the Master any further? Mark 5:23,35*

This was one desperate father. This was his last hope. His only hope. If she died while he was walking to Jesus, and the people from his house came with that message the situation must have been hopeless. The mourners were already in place. Why didn't he talk to Jesus when she first got sick? Why wait until there is no hope? He had a high position in the church and the church was not talking to Jesus at that time. Was he worried about what people would say then? Was he worried about how he would look, talking to Jesus? Jesus knew all of this, yet he went with him (when he was asked) to perform a miracle anyway. We can learn a few lessons from Jairus' story.

1. It's never too late to seek Jesus.

2. Don't let your position keep you from seeking Jesus.

3. If we turn to Jesus in our suffering, he won't turn us away, even if we could have sought him earlier.

4. Sometimes it is God that (seemingly) waits too late.

It is never too late to seek Jesus. Remember Nineveh? God had already pronounced judgement on this city, but they humbled themselves and repented and he turned his judgement around. What about the defeat at Ai? They were defeated by a small problem, but when they turned to the Lord and obeyed, God changed the outcome. God is for his people. He's not the harsh God that sits on his throne waiting to "zap" people, as some would have you believe. He is merciful, and full of compassion just waiting for us to want and need him.

Don't let your position keep you from seeking Jesus. Daniel was elevated to one of the highest offices in the land, but Daniel prayed three times a day. Daniel sought God daily as a government official and he had good success all the days of his life. And he was used mightily by God. David was the king of Israel. David sought the Lord continually. In battle, in worship and praise, day and night. It was David that exhorted us to meditate on God's word day and night.

If we turn to Jesus in our suffering, he won't turn us away, even if we could have sought him earlier.

> This is what the Sovereign LORD, the Holy One of Israel, says: "Only in returning to me and resting in me

> will you be saved. In quietness and confidence is your strength. But you would have none of it. You said, 'No, we will get our help from Egypt. They will give us swift horses for riding into battle.' But the only swiftness you are going to see is the swiftness of your enemies chasing you! So the LORD must wait for you to come to him so he can show you his love and compassion. For the LORD is a faithful God. Blessed are those who wait for his help. O people of Zion, who live in Jerusalem, you will weep no more. He will be gracious if you ask for help. He will surely respond to the sound of your cries. Though the Lord gave you adversity for food and suffering for drink, he will still be with you to teach you. You will see your teacher with your own eyes.
>
> Isaiah 30:15-16,18-20, NLT

God wants to be gracious to us and forgive us, and pour out blessings on us because he loves us. But first things first. We must repent. He won't put new wine into old wineskins. He needs us to turn to him in repentance so that he can do what only he can do, clean us up and make us fit for the blessings and graciousness he wants to pour into our lives.

But instead of turning to him we turn away to other things like alcohol, sex, shopping, entertainment, drugs, thinking these things will bring the relief from the negative consequences of trauma in our lives. And with arms open wide, God patiently awaits our return so that he can forgive us and begin the healing process. We have twisted the word of God and believe that we don't have to take part in our forgiveness. That God is so good that he just forgives us anyway. That we do not need to turn to him. Sometimes we think "it's too late, I've sinned and there's just no hope for me," but in those times we need to remember that God's ways are higher than our ways and his thoughts are not even like our thoughts. Turn to him anyway.

Sometimes it is God that (seemingly) waits too late.

When Abram was ninety-nine years old, the LORD appeared to him and said, "I am El-Shaddai—'God Almighty.' Serve me faithfully and live a blameless life… I will make you extremely fruitful. Your descendants will become many nations, and kings will be among them (Genesis 17:1,6 NLT).

Up to Abraham's time it was normal to have children at 90 years old. Ninety wasn't even considered old. But in Abraham's day somehow 90 was considered old. It was not normal to start a family at this age. But God's ways are not our ways. To accomplish his plan in our life he can go against culture, nature, or any organic or spiritual thing that gets in his way. He is "God Almighty." To Abraham it may have seemed that God waited too late to give him a child. Abraham was old, Sarah was old. "A baby?" How ridiculous at this time of life. But not only did they have a baby, after Sarah died, Abraham remarried and had more children. It's never too late to turn to God.

WALKING OUT GOD'S PLAN FOR US

The steps of a good man are ordered by the LORD: And he delighteth in his way. Though he fall, he shall not be utterly cast down: For the LORD upholdeth him with his hand
Psalm 37:23-24

If you are walking with the Lord, this "good man" is you. You are his child and he loves you. And just as a baby, when we were learning to walk, our father (or primary care giver) would watch over us carefully. And even though sometimes we would take a tumble, they were there to guard us and catch us so that the fall didn't harm us. They wouldn't let us fall down stairs, or land on concrete or rocks. They were standing by to protect us. And God is better than our earthly caretakers. We may fall into various temptations and struggles, but we will not be "utterly cast down." One translation says "we won't stay down." And another, says "we won't be there for long." And still another translates "utterly cast down" into "hurled," which means thrown with great force (with the intention of causing harm or damage). The word "utterly" means *absolutely, completely, or to the core*. So, we see here that our falls are not an attempt by our Father to demolish us, but only the things within us that need to be demolished. The enemy may mean it to bring us to a complete end, but God is there holding us by the hand, walking us through it. Just as he did with the Hebrew boys in the fiery furnace. The king said, "we threw in three, but I see four, and the fourth one looks just like the son of God." Just as he walked beside the disciples on their way to Emmaus. Their sorrow lifted as they walked with him and talked with him. And if you will turn to God in your sorrow, and walk with him, and talk with him, even though you don't understand the pain, he will lift it.

As we mature in Christ there are times we will have to *walk out* God's plans for our lives. We may feel alone or lonely while walking out the plan, but he left words of encouragement all over the Bible to strengthen us in our walk. He told us: he would not put more on us than we could bear (1 Corinthians 10:13). He would be with us (Isaiah 43:5 Psalm 23). He has plans for peace (shalom) and not evil (Jeremiah 29:11). And as our days, so shall our strength be (Deuteronomy 33:25). He will never leave us nor forsake us (Heb 13:5, Deuteronomy 4:31 Deuteronomy 31:6,8, Joshua 1:5, 1 Chronicles 28:20, Psalm 9:10). He would bind up our wounds (Psalm 147:3).

God made this promise to his children through the prophet Isaiah to encourage them as they were walking through a long period of suffering at the hands of their enemies:

> I have long time holden my peace; I have been still, and refrained myself: now will I cry like a travailing woman; I will destroy and devour at once. I will make waste mountains and hills, and dry up all their herbs; and I will make the rivers islands, and I will dry up the pools. And I will bring the blind by a way that they knew not; I will lead them in paths that they have not known: I will make darkness light before them, and crooked things straight. These things will I do unto them, and not forsake them. Isaiah 42:14-16

At times it may seem like God is just sitting around twiddling his thumbs while we suffer as if he just doesn't care about what is happening to us. However, you can rest assured that he does care and in his time he will act. In these times he often gives a promise. Sometimes he just has to hold himself back from rescuing us. Sometimes it's because we're not ready. Either we haven't changed our thinking enough to turn to him, or we're just not ready to believe he can do all the things he has promised he will do. Or, it could be as simple as we just didn't ask. So, he waits and we are confused. In Psalm 23:2b God is leading by *the still waters*, and 3b he is *leading in paths of righteousness*. How is it that in the very next verse we are walking through the valley of *the shadow of death* and evil is present? God is still there. It says so. It says, *"for thou art with me."* Have you ever been confused while walking with God? Why does he lead some to still refreshing waters, and righteous paths, but some of us have to pray that he doesn't lead us into temptation? Even when my mind is confused and I'm asking these questions, my heart is saying: "Your grace is sufficient for me; Your strength is made perfect in my weakness." "LORD, I put my trust in You." "I will bless you at all times, your praises shall continually be in my MOUTH." "Great is thy faithfulness." "Your mercies are new every morning." "You are my hiding place." No matter what my mind says, it's what my mouth and my heart say that counts. Because "out of the abundance of the heart the mouth *speaks*" (Matthew 12:34b). The mind is part of the flesh. It's going back to the dust. Let it ask it's questions, but let your heart and your mouth speak the praises of God only. God, your redeemer. *He redeemeth thy life from destruction* (Psalm 103:4a).

Lamentations 3:24 says: *"the LORD* (The Self-Existent One) *is my portion, saith my soul, therefore will I hope in Him."* This means the *self-existent one* is my allotment, inheritance, and all I have left. When I lose everything else in life that ever meant anything to me, if I have the LORD, the "I Am," the one who exists because of himself—who is God all by Himself—I have everything I need.

And the ending of the 23rd Psalm says: *"And I will dwell in the house of the LORD forever."* Leading me to the understanding that like the writer of Hebrews says *"through faith and patience (*we) *inherit* *the promises (6:12).* Stay the course. Endure. Don't give up. There's a crown of life waiting for you. God sees you and loves you. He loves *all* of you. Your faults, your failings, your down you, your up you. Isaiah 43:1 declares: *"But now, O Jacob, listen to the Lord who created you. O Israel, the one who formed you says, Do not be afraid, for I have ransomed you. I have called you by name; you are mine."* Notice how he calls him Jacob and Israel in the same sentence? That's because God recognizes that we are all two people. We are Jacob (un-regenerated) and we are Israel (Princes with God). He loves all of us. The total package. He loves us when we are bad, and he loves us when we are good. Because he knows that we really can't even be good without him.

God really does love you that much. He loved us enough to pay the ransom to purchase our souls. You don't pay a ransom for something you don't care about. No one can hold anything hostage that the other party doesn't care about. But when someone is dear to you, wouldn't you go to any length to pay the ransom for them? Peter emphasized how precious was the price paid for our souls:

> For you know that God paid a ransom to save you from the empty life you inherited from your ancestors. And it was not paid with mere gold or silver, which lose their value. It was the precious blood of Christ, the sinless, spotless Lamb of God. God chose him as your ransom long before the world began, but now in these last days he has been revealed for your sake.
>
> 1 Peter 1:18-20, NLT

We were so valuable to God that he paid the price with his own blood in the form of Jesus Christ. Keep taking your struggle to God. Be faithful to him and to his plan for your life. And WHEN (not if) it's all over you will say like David: *"it is good that I have been afflicted"* (Psalm 119:71).

Chapter Nine

Though

"Though you have made me see troubles, many and bitter, you will restore my life again; from the depths of the earth you will again bring me up." Psalm 71:20, NIV

"Though I walk in the midst of trouble, thou wilt revive me: thou shalt stretch forth thine hand against the wrath of mine enemies, and thy right hand shall save me." Psalm 138:7

For which cause we faint not; but though our outward man perish, yet the inward man is renewed day by day. 2 Corinthians 4:16

Though: even if, *in spite of, in spite of the fact*. Without being affected by the particular factor mentioned. Another way to say it is *"notwithstanding"*, *not standing with the facts*. The facts are over here, happening right now, but *though* says I don't have to stand with them. And moreover, God is not standing with them. He's standing with me. He supersedes the facts. He is Emmanuel, God with us. The facts say there is a valley of the shadow of death, and I am walking through it. But *though* says it doesn't matter. The facts say there is trouble, and I am walking in the midst of it. But *though* says it doesn't matter. Job said: *"And though after my skin worms destroy this body, yet in my flesh shall I see God" (Job 19:26)*. In other words, "it doesn't matter what happens to me in this body, in this world, I still have a God that loves me and I will see him in peace one day."

Yea, though I walk through the valley of the shadow of death, I will fear no evil: for thou art with me;...(23:4a) So what if evil comes against me? God is with me. He's on my side and I do not have to fear. I just have to run to him. The more evil that comes, the more I run to him, and hide in him, and lean on him, and let him be my strength.

He truly is a very present help in the time of trouble. Notice he said "Yea, though…." Yea means yes. Yes, often accompanies though. If you can say *though*, you can say *yes* to whatever comes.

Psalm 27:3 states, *"Though an host should encamp against me, my heart shall not fear: though war should rise against me, in this will I be confident (or, I will remain confident).* Remain confident in what? That the "LORD," the Self-Existent One, God all by himself and exists because of himself, is my light and salvation. Yes, the Lord is my happiness and everything I need to make me happy. He's my friend. He's the light of life. The Lord is the one who created the light. Not just visible light but the light of prosperity and the light of instruction. He provides illumination for every step I take so that I don't have to walk in darkness and need not stumble. But if I do stumble, he is my salvation, my deliverance, safety, and welfare. He comes to my rescue. Who wouldn't be confident in that?

"Stand therefore, having your loins girt about with truth…" (Ephesians 6:14). The first thing needed to stand is truth. The facts don't always speak the truth, only God's word does. Go to the word of God to find the truth, in the truth you will find your *though*. *And ye shall know* (absolutely understand) *the truth, and the truth shall make* (Liberate, deliver, unrestrained, to go at pleasure as a citizen and not a slave, exemption from obligation or liability) *you free (John 8:32).* While we are in the fight it's easier to believe the lies because that's what it has always looked like. But since we walk by faith and not by sight, we have to deny the lie and get in God's Word and say what He says about us, and about our situations. Facts don't matter much in the scheme of things: What the bank account says, what people think about me, what my health looks like, what I'm feeling at a given moment. However, what does matter are God's truths about me—those "thoughs." God's truths about me are discovered in his character and his character is revealed in his word. Read the word of God! It says the truth about who you are, who God is, how he feels about you, and how you should feel about yourself.

The Jewish people have an understanding that two truths can exist at the same time. On the one hand God is with us *"...and they shall call his name Emmanuel, which being interpreted is, God with us"(Matthew 1:23)*. But you say how can I be suffering so much if God is with me? On the other hand, there are lessons we need to learn, and he has to step back a little for us to learn them. We learn through the things we suffer. All beings learn that way. Even Jesus, God in flesh, learned obedience through the things he suffered. We (God's Children) should not be dissuaded by facts. Paul wasn't. Here is what Paul declared as he accepted the perils that would befall him if he went to Jerusalem.

> And now, behold, I go bound in the spirit unto Jerusalem, not knowing the things that shall befall me there: Save that the Holy Ghost witnesseth in every city, saying that bonds and afflictions abide me. But none of these things move me, neither count I my life dear unto myself, so that I might finish my course with joy, and the ministry, which I have received of the Lord Jesus, to testify the gospel of the grace of God. Acts 20:22-24

Paul was not moved by the predictions of suffering if he moved in the will of God to fulfill his assignment in Jerusalem. He said: though the facts say I will suffer I will not be deterred from the course of life I must walk. My life doesn't belong to me anymore, it belongs to the God that has called me to do his will. If it is his will for me to do a thing, then I am going to do that thing in spite of any facts that try to dissuade me.

Job wasn't. He said, *"Though he slay me yet will I trust him" (Job 13:15)*. Oh yes, Job had questions. He was mighty confused by the facts. He was crushed by the facts. He even got angry with the facts, but his mouth uttered *though*. A phrase of worship. Kryptonite to the devil and music to God's ears. Even the onslaught from his wife, his lifelong partner was unable to dissuade him.

The Hebrew boys were not dissuaded they said, *"If it be so, our God whom we serve is able to deliver us from the burning fiery furnace, and he will deliver us out of thine hand, O king" (Dan 3:17)*. In other words,

"Though you throw us in a fiery furnace, we don't care! Our God is able to deliver us. And if he doesn't, we still won't bow to you. We *will not* bow down to the things that displease our God! We still know the truth, that he is able, that he loves us and he is good! He is sovereign and can do whatever he pleases, and we will still serve him and not you!"

Mary was not dissuaded by the facts that if she were found to be pregnant before she and Joseph were legally married, she could be stoned to death. In those days it was criminal to have a child out of wedlock, actually a capital offense. She told the Angel of the Lord, *"be it unto me according to thy word" (Luke 1:38).* Mary had already counted up the cost and said YES! All Hebrew women wanted to be the mother of the Messiah. But not like this! It wasn't supposed to be this way. They had their own idea of how it would happen—Marriage, baby, fame. Though the scripture said *a Virgin would be with child* they just couldn't believe it could happen that way. Just like us. The Bible clearly says some things, but we choose to believe it's going to happen the way we think. We can't believe it's God's will that we suffer. Sometimes it is God that leads us into temptation. He doesn't tempt us, but he can lead us into temptation. Jesus even told us to pray that he wouldn't. God answers prayers the way he wants to, in his timing, and it's usually different than what we think (using a tree to heal bitter waters, babies in old age, taking people through a wilderness to freedom, using children as prophets).

The Hebrew word for *virgin* can also be translated *young girl* or *young woman*. In those days most women married very young. Mary was probably around 14 years old when she was espoused to Joseph. She was devout, (she knew the scriptures) women were not instructed in the Scriptures and yet Mary was able to quote the prophets. Mary may not have contemplated the totality of what she was about to go through, but she had a very good idea about how the first part would cause much suffering. As a matter of fact, it seems she had trouble figuring out how to tell Joseph and her parents because the Bible says Mary was "found to be with child" (Matthew 1:18). Can you say yes to suffering? Can you agree with God's plan for your life even though it may take you through the valley of the shadow of death?

Joseph was not dissuaded by the fact that if he took Mary to be his wife after finding her with child, he would be looked down upon in society and could possibly lose business by being ostracized by "religious" people. Nor was he dissuaded by the doubts that could assault his mind after committing to this marriage. He was not dissuaded by the fact that he would be a "stepfather" to a child that he knew he did not sire. He wasn't dissuaded by the possibility of gossip and wagging tongues, the extra mouth to feed before he and his spouse even had a proper honeymoon. What about the daunting responsibility of raising the Son of God? *Though* in spite of all the facts, Joseph took Mary to be his wife.

Though is a powerful weapon to use against the enemy. "The weapons of our warfare are not carnal. They are mighty through God…" (2 Corinthians 10:4 paraphrase). God teaches us how to fight and win. How do you think David felled a giant with a rock and a rag? Or Gideon saved Israel with his army of men bearing trumpets and flashlights? How did Sampson slay 1000 men with the jawbone of an ass? What did Elijah even use to kill 400 prophets of Baal? So, tell me, what can the enemy of our soul do when we say *"though He slay me, yet will I trust Him!"*

So…

Along with *though*, there is *so*. The word *so* has many meanings. It can be used as a command as in, *"Let the redeemed of the Lord say so…" (Psalms 107:2)*. It can be used to include, as in, *"Jesus got up and went with him, and so did his disciples" (Mat 9:19)*. It can be used to indicate "that is what happened" as in, And God said, *"Let the waters under the heaven be gathered together unto one place, and let the dry land appear: and it was so" (Genesis 1:9)*. And it can be used to indicate an extreme such as, "God *so* loved the world…" (John 3:16). It's the *so* in God *so* loved the world that gets me. The word *so* is an adverb that describes the love God has for us. It emphasizes the love he has. It's a great love. An intense love. An intentional love. It says God loved the world *to a great extent, extremely*. It's that extreme love that held him to the cross, and that same extreme love binds my heart to his. Even when I am going through a storm, especially when I am in a storm, it's that extreme love that anchors my soul, and provides a cradle of comfort for me to ride out the waves of intense emotions that try to demolish my faith in the One who loves me so.

So, can mean *therefore, consequently* or *subsequently*. So can abbreviate, indicate, or explicate. So, is absolutely an amazing word! *"Let the redeemed of the Lord say so."* In this context so means *I agree. I agree* that God is awesome, and I am redeemed by him. *I agree* that he is Alpha and Omega and that whatever he does in my life is right. *I agree* that his ways are higher than my ways and his thoughts are not like mine. *I agree* that I belong to him. I am his and he is mine and I trust him completely!

So, where did these people get the faith to stand? How did their *though* turn into *so*? They knew their God, and they agreed with him. *"...(B)ut the people that do know their God shall be strong, and do exploits" (Daniel 11:32b).* Knowing God's character will help you stand through anything the enemy can throw at you. That's why no weapon will prosper, it won't prosper because your faith is anchored in him that is able to do exceedingly abundantly above all we can ask or think (Eph. 3:20). But it's dependent upon the power that works in us. And we get that power through the knowledge of God. To know God intimately means we have relationship with him. Being in relationship with the Omnipotent changes the way we see life and the way we go through life. This is why we are able to do great things (exploits) because of the change brought about through suffering and being in relationship with him.

PROCESS, TIME, AND GRACE: THREE THINGS ABOUT SUFFERING

"And in process of time it came to pass, that Cain brought of the fruit of the ground an offering unto the Lord" (Genesis 4:3).

"Joshua waged war against all these kings for a long time" (Joshua 11:18, NIV).

Victory does not happen overnight. From the beginning God's way has always been process, time, and grace. God created process before creating time. The book of Genesis recounts that before God created time he set up the process of reproduction. After that he created time.

> Then God said, "Let the land sprout with vegetation-every sort of seed-bearing plant, and trees that grow seed-bearing fruit. These seeds will then produce the kinds of plants and trees from which they came." And that is what happened. Then God said, "Let lights appear in the sky to separate the day from the night. Let them be signs to mark the seasons, days, and years. Genesis 1:11,14, NLT

Then, after creating mankind he told them to be fruitful and multiply, knowing it takes nine months to make a baby and years for the children to grow old enough to reproduce. Even with multiple births he knew it would be a long process to populate the earth. But God knows the end from the beginning, so he waited. Malachi proclaimed that *"God sits as the refiner and purifier of silver" (3:3)* That job takes a lot of patience, purifying silver is a process. God has the patience to sit and watch as his plans and processes unfold in the earth. God, the creator forms his creation to do his will. *"But now thus saith the Lord that created thee, O Jacob, and he that formed thee, O Israel," (Isaiah 43:1a)*. God created Jacob the man but formed Israel. This denotes process. To become who and what God called you to be, you will go through the process.

"By little and little I will drive them out from before thee, until thou be increased, and inherit the land" (Exodus 23:30).

God is a god of process. He processes us on every level. We may fight the same devil, but we fight on different levels as we grow. However, to us it just feels the same because we are in it. So, the faith to move on after the issue becomes *the* issue. And stepping out on that faith leads to new levels. Just like the Children of Israel trying to possess the promised land, the issue was fighting for it to take it from those who possessed it. After that the new issue was driving out the beasts that were there after they drove out the people. All they knew was that they were fighting. They didn't realize that they were fighting on new levels. Fighting beasts is different than fighting people yet it was still a fight. Sometimes we are prospering and don't know it. Just like we age, grow taller, get bigger. From our perspective, some things are not perceptible. Others can see it but unless we stop and contemplate, we have a difficult time seeing it for ourselves. Sometimes we just have to take a step back to get an understanding that the process is working.

Grace and truth came through Jesus Christ. However, even he had to go through the process to be born as a man on this earth. He had to sit in his mother's womb and grow into a fertilized egg to a blastocyst to a fetus to fully formed baby. His toes had to be formed. His fingers had to be formed. Hair was planted in his scalp, just like everyone else. He took the exact same period of nine months to grow in her belly as we grew in someone else's. It was process. Oh, how he understood process.

As Jesus walked the earth, amongst his creation, he continued to use process, even in the midst of working a miracle. At the wedding in Cana of Galilee when his mother asked him for a miracle because they had run out of wine, Jesus responded by telling them to: *"Fill the waterpots with water. And they filled them up to the brim. And he saith unto them, Draw out now, and bear unto the governor of the feast. And they bare it" (John 2:7-8)*. Jesus used process. He could have turned the water into wine straight from the well where they had to draw it from first. But he didn't. The Bible is very particular in the description of the water pots and yet in reading that scripture we often miss the inference. We don't normally realize that this in-depth description telling us about these stone water pots is inferring time and process. Granted, it was less time than it normally takes to make wine from grapes, yet there was still time and process involved. He told them to go to the well, do the hard work of sending down a bucket and bringing it back to this stone water pot over and over again until this large pot was filled. The pots were made of stone, and they were large enough to contain 20-30 gallons of water. Therefore, we can assume that they did not take the water pots to the well, but instead were forced to go to the well over and over with smaller containers they could carry. How many servants did it take and how much time to fill six of these large water pots? That would have been 120-180 gallons of water in stone water pots. That's a lot of trips to the well and back. Over and over again.

They didn't have a kitchen with running water or a water hose they could bring to the stone pots. Unless they had a nearby source of water they had to travel over and over and over again to the well, fill a smaller bucket, bring it back, pour it into the larger stone pot until it was full. This was a process, and it took some time and effort. Yet even with that, it still took a miracle to turn that water into wine. Jesus didn't do the process, he ordered the people to do that, but he did do what they could not do. God will not do for us what we can do for ourselves, no matter how long it takes us to do it.

For instance:

> Now when Pharaoh had let the people go, God did not lead them by the way of the land of the Philistines, even though it was near; for God said, "The people might change their minds when they see war, and return to Egypt." Hence God led the people around by the way of the wilderness to the Red Sea...(Exodus 13:17-18, NASB).

God is all powerful, couldn't he have miraculously given them courage to fight? He could have. But God is a good father. A good father teaches his children by allowing natural consequences to help his children learn valuable lessons that they will need to carry them through life. A good father allows his children to gain autonomy through struggle as he carefully watches to step in when truly needed. God is a good Father.

This pattern of process and time can be seen throughout the scriptures. Notice words like "it came to pass," or "in the process of time."

Or you may notice time and process in the middle of scriptures such as: *"The steps (process) of a good man are ordered by the Lord: and he delighteth in his way (process)"* (Psalms 37:23). And, *"God's way is perfect. All the Lord's promises prove true..."* (*2 Samuel 22:31a, NLT*). His ways prove to be true. It takes time to prove something. This denotes process. Sometimes we just have to walk out the promises he gave us, because with the promise comes an inner knowing that his word will prove to be true. We don't have to see it or feel it. We just know it. The enemy will always come along side us to make us think it will not happen. But if you wait, his promises always prove true.

"But in that coming day..." (Isaiah 54:17a) more words that reveal process and time. These words come just before some words everyone knows and quotes. That *"no weapon formed against me shall prosper."* Everyone loves those words, but I love *"but in that coming day"* so much more. Those words speak of hope of the good that is to come. They tell me that this night will end and daylight and all the goodness that comes with it is on the way. Hope!

"Your eyes saw my unformed substance, and in Your book all the days [of my life] were written before ever they took shape, when as yet there was none of them." (Psalm 139:16, AMPC).

Now this is so hard to swallow when I am in the midst of suffering. I want to scream, "okay God, if you knew I was going to suffer like this, then why didn't you do something? Why are you sitting back watching this painful mess unfold? Don't you care?" Then I am reminded of the disciples asking that same question in the midst of their storm. But Jesus did care. You see not only did he see them going into the storm, and struggling in the midst of the storm, he also saw them coming out of the storm with a stronger faith and more substance than when they went in. Yes, God knows all about your suffering, but he also sees "that coming day." So, keep your faith in the storm. Not only does he care, but he is with us. Jesus was with the disciples on the ship in the storm and he is with us. They named him *Immanuel* which is God with us. The "dwell amongst us God." So, *"Trust in the Lord with all your heart." "With all your heart"* means to gather everything within you to believe. Believe what? That he is good, that he is sovereign, that he loves you and is able to and willing to work it all out for your good. Yes, good is the *"expected end"* Jeremiah 29:11 talks about.

In the book of Exodus, God came down to deliver his people. The process began by talking to Moses the one he chose to lead his people out of bondage. But this was only the beginning of the long process of deliverance. Sometimes when we think of deliverance we think immediate, but God is thinking process. He has a plan. First, he had to convince an unwilling leader, next that leader had to convince the people. Then Moses had to convince Pharaoh. After all of this convincing the actual implementation of the plan came. And the people were delivered "from" bondage but the process wasn't over until they were delivered "to" the promised land. This exemplifies process, time, and grace.

May God give you more and more grace and peace as you grow in your knowledge of God and Jesus our Lord (2 Peter 1:2, NLT. Still talking about process here. Peter is trying to tell us that as our knowledge of God grows so will our grace. We will learn to give others grace more and more as our knowledge of our Heavenly Father and his earthy son grows; and we will also understand how to give grace to ourselves. Both are needed to be whole in Christ. Grace begets peace. Peace with others and peace with ourselves. Grace and peace are essential for unity, and when we achieve unity we can do anything we set our hearts to. The words "as you grow" denotes process. It is a process to attain the knowledge that brings about this kind of grace and peace. It takes grace to suffer. When Paul was suffering from the thorn in his flesh (the messenger of Satan that was sent to buffet him) after praying three times for God to remove it, he learned that God's grace was sufficient for him. God's strength is made perfect in our weakness (2 Cor. 12:7).

PART II

Comfort, Peace, and Inspiration

Be of Good Cheer

On that day the announcement to Jerusalem will be, "Cheer up, Zion! Don't be afraid! For the LORD your God is living among you. He is a mighty savior. He will take delight in you with gladness. With his love, he will calm all your fears. He will rejoice over you with joyful songs." "I will gather you who mourn for the appointed festivals; you will be disgraced no more. And I will deal severely with all who have oppressed you. I will save the weak and helpless ones; I will bring together those who were chased away. I will give glory and fame to my former exiles, wherever they have been mocked and shamed. On that day I will gather you together and bring you home again. I will give you a good name, a name of distinction, among all the nations of the earth, as I restore your fortunes before their very eyes. I, the LORD, have spoken!"
Zephaniah 3:16-20, NLT

God delights in soothing our doubts and calming our fears. After he has tried us. After we have come through the fire and stood the test of time he swoops in to bring encouragement and comfort. In the first section we attempted to bring some clarity to the fact that we suffer. To identify some of the reasons we suffer and some of the ways we suffer. In this next section I will be attempting to impart to you the comfort wherewith God has comforted me in all my trials and tests. This section has no particular rhyme or reason, just to comfort you and bring you peace in the midst of your time of tribulation. To let you know that you are not alone and that you can find fellowship in your suffering. So, feel free to read this section in any order you wish, consecutively or by skipping to the chapter you feel most identifies with your pain. As long as you are ministered to and receive the hope infused back into your soul that may have seeped out due to suffering.

THE PROMISE

By: Cynthia Gibson-Dyse

How could they bear being driven from the garden?

They had a promise!

How could he preach of a flood unseen?

He had a promise!

How could he uproot all that he owned

And set out for a city as yet unknown?

He had a promise!

How could he offer up his only son

When God had told him "this is the one?"

He had a promise!

How could he accept his lot in life,

Hated by his brothers and Potiphar's wife?"

He had a promise!

How could he refuse the life of a pharaoh,

Giving up pleasure for work and sorrow?

He had a promise!

They crossed the Red Sea

As if it were dry land.

And when Jericho fell

Called To Suffer

Why did Rahab's house stand?

They had a promise!

They were beaten and mocked,

Imprisoned in chains.

Tormented, persecuted, enduring great pain.

Wandering in deserts, mountains and caves;

Not accepting relief

So the soul could be saved.

Why?

They had a promise!

He went to the cross to suffer and die.

He paid the full cost and I'll tell you why…

He WAS the Promise!

Chapter Ten

The Promise

"Remember those earlier days after you had received the light, when you endured in a great conflict full of suffering. Sometimes you were publicly exposed to insult and persecution; at other times you stood side by side with those who were so treated. You suffered along with those in prison and joyfully accepted the confiscation of your property, because you knew that you yourselves had better and lasting possessions. So do not throw away your confidence; it will be richly rewarded. You need to persevere so that when you have done the will of God, you will receive what he has promised."
Hebrews 10:32-36, NIV

God loves to encourage the sufferer. Wherever you see suffering in the Bible, look closer, you'll see a loving God standing there waiting to be gracious. Only a good God would even think to give us a promise so that we would have something to hold on to. That's why he does it. He knows how painful and nasty the middle can get on the way to our expected end. So, he gives us a promise. Promises are sweet little somethings whispered into our ears to ease the pain of what tomorrow will bring.

All the promises in the Bible came because someone he loved was suffering and he wanted to assure them that they were going to be ok. Where there is a promise there's usually a problem. As I read through the Bible, I often wondered how the people in those times were able to cope with all the pain and suffering I saw, until I realized, they had a promise. From Adam to the last church age there is a promise connected to all the suffering. But the most important thing to remember is that THE promise dwells amongst us and is with us always. Jesus was the promise. The greatest promise. Our portion.

There are many promises in the Bible. Some of them make us glad. We look forward to them. We hope for them. And as the psalmist said we watch for them more than they that watch for the morning (Psalm 130:6). But what do we do with those promises that don't make us feel good? Because along with all the promises of good and hope are promises of suffering and even anguish. But somehow we tend to overlook those, or are we hiding from them like we did when we were a child? A child will hide in plain sight and close its eyes believing if he can't see you then you can't see him. Or like an ostrich who sticks its head in the sand to hide from the enemy. But we can't just close our eyes or hide from what we don't like and make it go away. There are promises of suffering in the Bible. But even behind the promises we like hides the fact that if there is a promise, there is a problem. A promise implies that there is a problem. There would be no reason to promise anything if there were no problem to remedy. So, in answer to our problems God gives promises. Someone has to be weak and powerless in order for God to promise to give strength. You have to be the poor and needy to receive a promise that your needs will be met. You have to be sick in order to receive the promise of healing. You have to be in trouble to receive a promise of deliverance. Why would God promise something not needed? We like to claim the promises without going through the problem. But the promises of God (good or bad) are "yea and amen."

Oh, the precious promises of God. Like Deuteronomy 33:27-29 declares,

> The eternal God is thy refuge, and underneath are the everlasting arms: and he shall thrust out the enemy from before thee; and shall say, Destroy them. Israel then shall dwell in safety alone: the fountain of Jacob shall be upon a land of corn and wine; also his heavens shall drop down dew. Happy art thou, O Israel: who is like unto thee, O people saved by the Lord, the shield of thy help, and who is the sword of thy excellency! and thine enemies shall be found liars unto thee; and thou shalt tread upon their high places.   Deuteronomy 33:27-29

This promise came after wandering through the wilderness for 40 years. All of the older original diaspora dying one by one. Although the Bible is a collection of books full of suffering, there are a myriad of promises attached to all the sufferings. And God's promises always prove true, they are yea and amen. When David was delivered from the hand of Saul, his nemesis, he wrote this Psalm to God: *"God's way is perfect. All the Lord's promises prove true. He is a shield for all who look to him for protection" (Psalms 18:30, NLT)*. David spent many years running from his enemies and fighting God's enemies even though he had already been anointed to be king. Wait, I'm anointed to be king one day and the next I'm back tending sheep? And after that I'm still not king? I have to run from the current king? Then, when that king dies, I'm still not king? I have to fight my grown son over the crown? Wait, wasn't David a boy when he was anointed to be king? Now he has a grown son and he has not stepped into his promise? Yet he's writing a poem about how God's promises always prove true.

David was an expert at encouraging himself. He had to be. He was trained in the fields with the sheep. While tending sheep he was able to get away from the family that disliked him. His brothers put him down constantly, and his father hated him. David had to learn to encourage himself then so that when he became a leader and his men wanted to stone him because their families were abducted by the enemy, David didn't yield to self-pity, he encouraged himself in the Lord. The self-existent one. David knew his God, intimately. He recognized the sovereignty and authority of God, and he wrote about it often. He knew that his help came from God and God alone. He knew that it was good to be afflicted, because when we turn to God in our afflictions, our afflictions shape us into who God wants us to be. I had to learn these lessons also in the fiery furnace of afflictions that what I was going into was not what I was going to be. I learned that I am what I am, because of what I was.

I Am What I Am Because of What I Was

By: Cynthia Gibson-Dyse

I am what I am because of what I was.

I was a leaf shaking in the wind.

Every breeze moved me,

Every storm shook me

Every ray of sun changed my colors.

Every bug dined on me,

Every drop of rain drenched me,

Every curious hand ripped me from my source.

I was a leaf shaking in the wind.

But I went down to the valley of the shadow of death and became.

I became a tree that would not shake,

That would not move

That would not break.

That would not be dined on, reclined on

A tree that the sun always shined on.

I could not be swept away by the rain,

No curious hand could cause me pain.

I became a tree planted by the waters

Stretching forth my branches,

Cynthia Gibson-Dyse

Giving shade to others.

I am what I am

Because of what I was.

Chapter Eleven

Called to Greatness

When you are called to suffer, it's because you're called to greatness. You never come through suffering the same as you went in. You will come out better, or bitter. You come out better by leaning into the one who loves you. He knows what he is doing. He really does. 1 Peter 4:1 tells us to "arm ourselves to suffer" just as Christ suffered. God will prepare us in various ways to go through a difficult time. I recall in the Bible when he called the virgin Mary to bear his son, he sent an angel to speak to her, to grant him permission to use the body he had created. Why? Because he knew that when she agreed to the plan he had she would need the knowledge that God himself was on her side. She needed a promise. When God sends angels to talk to you, or talks to you himself, you are about to go through something! Remember Jonah, Abraham, Moses, Noah? After their encounter with God in various ways, they went through.

I know this because it happened to me. I am not one of those people who claims God speaks to them all the time but, I did have an encounter with him in my prayer room as a young mother in an abusive marriage. I was fasting and praying in my prayer closet early one morning, and I was on my knees reading my Bible when the Lord took me to the 54th chapter of Isaiah. As I read, it was if the voice of God was reading it to me and it was all about me. This poor woman who was dealing with terrible shame, who was bereft of her children and hated by her husband. A wife of youth dealing with loss, grief, shame, and despair. A woman who felt forsaken and alone. But God encountered me in that prayer room and gave me promises that I still hold onto today. And even though over 30 years later I have not seen the total manifestation of the whole, I still believe. Because I have seen some down payments. I have seen parts of my personal promise come to pass which in turn gives me the faith to believe I will see the entire promise fulfilled if I stay in faith. *Blessed is she who has believed that the Lord would fulfill his promises to her!" (Luke 1:45 NIV) For no word from God will ever fail (Luke 1:37 NIV)*. Mary, the mother of Jesus learned this. As she rubbed her pregnant belly in her lonely room, she knew she had not been with a man, and yet she was with child just like the angel said. Therefore, if one part of a prophesy or promise from God comes true, the rest is true also, and we can cling to the rest and watch for it more than they that watch for the morning. Why? Because when God says something, we can take it to the bank. We can stand on his word when things look opposite what he said.

ALL I NEED IS HIS WORD

By: Cynthia Gibson-Dyse

He promised that he would do it for me

So all I need is His word.

No matter how hard the problem may be,

All I need is His word.

He parted the waters of the mighty Red Sea

All I need is His word.

If He did it for them, He can do it for me

All I need is His word.

He brought water from the rock at the river's banks

All I need is His word.

So all I have to do is give Him thanks

Because all I need is His word.

I'm not worried about the problem

Because God is able.

He puts clothes on my back and food on my table.

He protected me from the raging storm.

Nothing's too hard for my God to perform!

All I need is His word.

Chapter Twelve

Fully Persuaded

"And being fully persuaded that, what he had promised, he was able also to perform."
Romans 4:21

Fully persuaded. You ask me how I became fully persuaded? By waiting on the Lord. By watching him show me that he is God all by himself. When we start out walking with God we are full of faith and full of strength and hope. But somewhere along the way we encounter disappointment, discouragement, and sometimes even hopelessness. But when we take these emotions to God and don't turn away from him we learn how to wait. And in our waiting God is working. As we turn to him in sorrow his Spirit binds us in his love (because God is love), and the waiting turns into renewed strength. This is a strength that cannot be shaken by the external.

Mostly we get shaken because we have not counted up the cost of living in the Kingdom of God. Jesus said (actually warned): *"If any man come to me, and hate not his father, and mother, and wife, and children, and brethren, and sisters, yea, and his own life also, he cannot be my disciple. And whosoever doth not bear his cross, and come after me, cannot be my disciple. So likewise, whosoever he be of you that forsaketh not all that he hath, he cannot be my disciple"* (Luke 14:26-27,33). Jesus let them know that there is a great cost to being his disciple. Have you counted the cost? Anything that is free is not valued. But when you pay a great price for something you value it.

"Therefore turn thou to thy God: keep mercy and judgment, and wait on thy God continually." Hosea 12:6

"For I am persuaded, that neither death, nor life, nor angels, nor principalities, nor powers, nor things present, nor things to come...." The NLT says it this way, *"neither our fears for today nor our worries about tomorrow...."* Not even the powers of hell can separate us from God's love. *"...Nor height, nor depth, nor any other creature, shall be able to separate us from the love of God, which is in Christ Jesus our Lord." Romans 8:38, 39*

What does it take to persuade someone? To be persuaded means someone or something changed your mind. It means they brought enough evidence to make you see a different point of view. God has a good track record of persuading his people. Gideon, Moses, Joshua, Joseph, his disciples. Sometimes when we are suffering we can only see our suffering from our point of view and not God's. This is what Jesus told Peter after Peter rebuked him for telling the disciples of his forthcoming suffering: *"Jesus turned to Peter and said, "Get away from me, Satan! You are a dangerous trap to me. You are seeing things merely from a human point of view, not from God's" (Matthew 16:23, NLT).*

Your perspective is your point of view. When your perception is messed up then your perspective will be skewed. In 2 Corinthians 12:9, God told Paul that his (God's) strength is made perfect in our weakness. Yet we often fight *not* to be weak. So, whose strength do you want to be glorified? You may need to ask God to help you to see your situation from his point of view. If you are blinded by your pain, your point of view is useless. It will only cause you more pain as you react in ways most humans do. But if you will look to the hills from whence cometh your help, you will find the author and finisher of your faith standing there waiting to assist you with all your needs. But he will not barge into your existence, you must invite him in. God's plans for us are perfect even when it entails suffering because he sits high and looks low and can always see the end from the beginning. One becomes fully persuaded by turning to God in times of trouble or testing instead of away from him. The more you turn to him in suffering the deeper your persuasion.

I can't even read my Bible without seeing all the suffering in it. As a social worker I see and hear about great suffering. In my daily life I can see in the news and social media great suffering of many. And yet I am not sad or discouraged. Because I have an intimate understanding of the character of God. Of his great power and his love for the world. My hope is built on a sure foundation, and I am fully persuaded.

Chapter Thirteen

He Redeems and Restores

*Who redeemeth thy life from destruction; who
crowneth thee with lovingkindness and tender mercies;
Psalm 103:4*

*"with great compassion I will take you back." "with everlasting love
I will have compassion on you," says the Lord, your Redeemer. "I will
never again be angry and punish you." "The mountains may move and
the hills disappear, but even then my faithful love for you will remain"
Isaiah 54:7b, 8b, 9b, 10a*

You can be stripped of everything except that which is the most precious thing—God's love. When God does the stripping, do not think it means he doesn't love you or that he isn't in control. God loves us with an everlasting love. It never ends. Just because from this side of heaven it feels like he has left us or he doesn't care about us or what we are going through, doesn't mean this is the truth. It just means we have to stand on his Word and his faithful promise to love us, to redeem us and keep us. A word that I have been able to stand on is: *"The Lord executeth righteousness and judgment for all that are oppressed" (Psalm 103:6)*. I stood on this word and he delivered me from many unfair situations by his power and righteousness. Sometimes I had to wait and sit in darkness, but sure deliverance did come.

In the second chapter of Joel, God had the prophet encourage his people with these words:

> Don't be afraid, you animals of the field, for the wilderness pastures will soon be green. The trees will again be filled with fruit; fig trees and grapevines will be loaded down once more. Rejoice, you people of Jerusalem! Rejoice in the Lord your God! For the rain he sends demonstrates his faithfulness. Once more the autumn rains will come, as well as the rains of spring. The threshing floors will again be piled high with grain, and the presses will overflow with new wine and olive oil.
>
> Joel 2:22-24, NLT

This passage speaks of hope of an expected end. It demonstrates such care that God has that he is even encouraging the animals of the field. Sometimes in the darkest times it can feel as if God doesn't care but the word of God declares his glory and his caring nature throughout. As we look at nature and see the patterns of death, burial and resurrection, we can be assured that when we are in our dark times, our "burial" God is faithful. And when the season cycles back around for resurrection, we will arise. Just as Micah said, *"when I fall, I shall arise; when I sit in darkness, the Lord shall be a light unto me (Micah 7:8b).*

Chapter Fourteen
Singing Through Your Pain

"Sing, O barren, thou that didst not bear; break forth into singing, and cry aloud, thou that didst not travail with child: for more are the children of the desolate than the children of the married wife, saith the Lord."
Isaiah 54:1

God commanded her to sing during one of the most painful grief-filled periods of her life. And he has commanded all his people to do the same. Psalm 66:1-2 commands:

> Shout joyful praises to God, all the earth! Sing about the glory of his name! Tell the world how glorious he is. NLT

And Psalms 67:5:-7 says:

> Let the people praise thee, O God; let all the people praise thee. Then shall the earth yield her increase; and God, even our own God, shall bless us. God shall bless us; and all the ends of the earth shall fear him.

When you are greatly suffering it's hard to lift up your head and sing praises and be joyful. And you might ask: "Why should I?" As my heart cries out in pain the questions that come to my mind when asked to sing are, What do I sing at a time like this? How can I sing at a time like this? Why should I sing at a time like this?

You see, being barren was a very painful thing for Jewish women back then. Because of God's promise to Eve every woman wanted to be the mother of the Messiah. The one who would bruise the serpent's head. Children were considered a blessing in that culture. They provided for parents in their old age. They helped with all the work that needed to be done. And most importantly they carried on the birthright and heritage of the family and the Faith. To not have any children was a disgrace and a very painful thing to bear. It's reminiscent of the time when the children of Israel were in Babylonian captivity and their captors were requiring them to sing the songs of Zion, and they refused. They hung up their harps and musical instruments and just wept (Psalm 137:1-4). So how could you ask me to sing knowing my past, and knowing what the future holds?

Exactly! God knows what your future holds. If you read further, you will see the plans of good and not evil God makes to this pain filled, shame filled woman. If you have lived long enough you already know that life never turns out the way we expected. And that can bring much disappointment and pain. But when we turn to God in our pain and disappointment, he holds our expectations in his hands, in his timing, and in his will. So, turn to him, rest in him and sing. When you turn to Jesus in your moments of suffering you can go deep into him. He can take you so deep in him that you find the comfort you need without anything changing externally. Jesus said in John 10:9: *I am the door: by me if any man enter in, he shall be saved, and shall go in and out, and find pasture.* "Finding Pasture" is another way of saying finding rest, nourishment, all your necessities met- "*Shalom.*"

"Then sang Moses and the children of Israel this song unto the Lord, and spake, saying, I will sing unto the Lord, for he hath triumphed gloriously: the horse and his rider hath he thrown into the sea" (Exodus 15:1).

The children of Israel sang and worshipped after God brought deliverance, but when the next thing went wrong they were murmuring and complaining again. It is proper to sing, and worship, and be thankful when God does something for you. You should keep doing that. But God gets glory when we sing and worship and thank him before he does it. While we're still having the problem. While we are still in pain. While the trouble is still showing up every day. Before he delivers. This is why he told her to sing, and this is why he wants us to sing.

"Sing unto the Lord, O ye saints of his, and give thanks at the remembrance of his holiness" (Psalm 30:4).

Expanded versions of this verse translates *holiness* into *holy name*. In the Hebrew culture a name is more than just what people call you, a name also represents your character traits. So, this verse instructs us to remember God's holy character and give thanks by singing. It is always good to remember all the things God has done for you, the big things and the little things. The ways he has brought you through and to praise him for those things. Thinking about the times you suffered but God was Emanuel, right there in it with you. Looking back, we can see the ways God made. This always makes me so grateful. Thinking about his goodness lifts my heart to heights of glory. I can't praise him enough. I can see his hand in my life and how his hand worked things for my good and my soul sings. David said: *"The Lord is my strength and my shield; my heart trusted in him, and I am helped: therefore my heart greatly rejoiceth; and with my song will I praise him" (Psalm 28:7).* When our hearts rejoice, we sing about his goodness. Singing about God's character can assist you in remembering his goodness. David praised God before trouble, through trouble, and after trouble was over. David was a man after God's heart.

"When evening came, the disciples came to Him and said, This is a remote and barren place, and the day is now over; send the throngs away into the villages to buy food for themselves. Jesus said, They do not need to go away; you give them something to eat. They said to Him, We have nothing here but five loaves and two fish" (Matthew 14:15-17, AMPC).

Jesus always asks more of us when we feel we have reached our limits. Just like he asked the barren woman to sing when he knew she was in great pain. He loves to bring life out of barren places. Hannah was barren but brought forth Samuel one of the greatest prophets ever. And after that brought forth five more children. Elizabeth was barren and brought forth another great prophet, John the Baptist. Sarah and Rachel were both barren, and from them God's Chosen people were born. God brought life from barrenness through women who turned to him and allowed him to use them. And after that there was great joy. Hannah even wrote a song.

Why sing? Because it is a structured way to drown out the negativity. Singing is an integral part of our worship. There are two entire books of the Bible dedicated to songs the *Psalms* and the book called the *Song of Songs*, or the *Song of Solomon*. The Bible admonishes us to sing psalms to God and talk of his wondrous works (1 Chronicles 16:9 and Psalm 105:2), and to come before his presence with singing (Psalm 96:2). In the book of Ephesians Paul tells us to speak to ourselves in psalms and hymns and spiritual songs. And to the Colossians he also said the same. James said we should sing if we are merry. The mountains trees and forests were even commanded to sing in Isaiah 44. Zephaniah even said God would "joy over us with singing." God was giving this pain filled woman a tool to deal with the pain in her heart. Singing is a powerful gift from God. You don't have to join a choir or sing in front of people. Just sing. If you can't get started turn on some worship music and join them. Sing until the pain subsides. Sing until your joy returns. Sing until the tears flow then sing until the tears dry up. Sing.

So, the answer to those questions are: *"Sing praises to God, sing praises: sing praises unto our King, sing praises" (Psalm 47:6).* "Sing unto God, ye kingdoms of the earth; O sing praises unto the Lord; Selah" (Psalm 68:32).* Sing with the strength he will provide,*" He giveth power to the faint; and to them that have no might he increaseth strength" (Isaiah 40:29).* Sing *because* he is good. *"Praise the Lord; for the Lord is good: sing praises unto his name; for it is pleasant" (Psalm 135:3).* God will provide the strength needed to sing, so sing. *"The Lord will give strength unto his people; the Lord will bless his people with peace" (Psalms 29:11).*

Chapter Fifteen
Little Strength

"because you know that these troubles test your faith, and this will give you patience."
James 1:3, NCV

Struggle + faith x experience = strength. As parents we often try to protect our children from the pain that comes with suffering. So, we advise them, lecture them, restrict them, coddle them, and we do everything in our power to protect them from the struggle. The problem is, by doing this we also deprive them of the end result of the feeling of victory, accomplishment, innovation and patience. God, on the other hand doesn't protect us from struggle, or suffering. Because God knows the end from the beginning he allows suffering, struggle, and pain, but he doesn't allow it to harm us. For his children the end result of struggle, suffering, and pain is victory.

Jesus rebuked Peter for trying to protect him from suffering. *"But he turned, and said unto Peter, Get thee behind me, Satan: thou art an offence unto me: for thou savourest not the things that be of God, but those that be of men" (Matthew 16:23).* This is the slap heard around the world. How angry do you think Peter was when he heard Jesus' rebuke? Didn't he just call Judas friend and Judas had just betrayed him? *How am I the devil?* Because the devil didn't want Jesus to take away the sins of the world, and he had to do it by suffering. The devil would love for us to live in ease if it will divert us from our purpose. Jesus came to earth to suffer and to shed his blood and die so that we might live. But sometimes others looking on think we are being dramatic, or mean, or acting like a victim, when we are suffering. But *au contraire*, the struggle is what makes us more than conquerors.

"Now thanks be unto God, which always causeth us to triumph in Christ, and maketh manifest the savour of his knowledge by us in every place" (2 Corinthians 2:14). In other words, when God causes us to triumph in tribulation, the knowledge of him begins to spread like a sweet-smelling perfume or a luscious bakery dessert. Savor equals aroma. And afterwards, after we have suffered, he brings restoration and healing. *"He restoreth my soul: he leadeth me in the paths of righteousness for his name's sake" (Psalm 23:3).* "He restoreth my soul" the *New Living Translation* renders it this way: *"he renews my strength."* However, that doesn't capture it like the *King James*. Strength could be talking about any strength, and that's okay, good even. But the soul is the mind, will, and emotions. When your soul is tired it takes a toll on your whole being, your essence. Some people call God the "Great Physician," but I say he's a surgeon. A great surgeon because he knows just where to touch, exactly where to cut and he goes to the exact place it hurts and is able to heal it miraculously with one word or one touch. He is so precise.

> The LORD helps the fallen and lifts those bent beneath their loads.   Psalm 145:14, NLT

He lifts so graciously and so faithfully.

> How blessed is the man whose strength is in You, In whose heart are the highways to Zion! Passing through the valley of Baca (weeping)they make it a spring; The early rain also covers it with blessings. They go from strength to strength, Every one of them appears before God in Zion.   Psalm 84:5-7, NASB

We pass through the hard times, the trauma that life brings. We come out on the other side with strength.

"Be not afraid of their faces: for I am with thee to deliver thee, saith the Lord" Jeremiah 1:8

Just because God is with us doesn't mean we won't suffer. But you can depend on his strength to see you through or deliver you. He told Jeremiah he would be with him, yet Jeremiah was called the weeping prophet. Jeremiah suffered. He had to go through all the suffering he prophesied to God's people and more. Because some kings couldn't deal with the truth they made Jeremiah suffer. God warned Jeremiah: *"And they shall fight against thee; but they shall not prevail against thee; for I am with thee, saith the Lord, to deliver thee" (Jeremiah 1:19)*. God was faithful to Jeremiah, and he will be faithful to us. To be with us in the time of tribulation, and strengthen us when we are weak.

> I will strengthen the weary and renew those who are weak. Jeremiah 31:25, CEB

> I know all the things you do, and I have opened a door for you that no one can close. You have little strength, yet you obeyed my word and did not deny me. Revelation 3:8, NLT

> But they that wait upon the Lord shall renew their strength; they shall mount up with wings as eagles; they shall run, and not be weary; and they shall walk, and not faint. Isaiah 40:31

Why would anyone faint from walking? Maybe the walk was too long and the end was far away? Maybe they were walking at the wrong pace? Or maybe they forgot to eat, and the weather was bad and they just lost strength. Do you see? Even when our strength is little we don't have to worry because God has all the strength we need and is willing to provide it for us. But he just doesn't provide it the way we think. He provides it through us getting back up every time we fall. *"The steps of a good man are ordered by the Lord: and he delighteth in his way. Though he fall, he shall not be utterly cast down: for the Lord upholdeth him with his hand" (Psalm 37:23-24)*.

Have you ever lifted weights or tried to do pushups or pull ups and couldn't get past the first one? I guarantee you (unless you have some kind of muscle disease) that if you kept at it you would build muscle to do more and more until you were pumping them out like a pro. This happened to me when I joined the army. I was 28 years old and was not into exercise. Before being assigned to a basic training unit each person had to show they were fit enough to do at least a certain number of pushups and sit ups that they required. I discovered how weak I was. I barely made the minimum to go to basic training. But in basic training every other day we did strength training exercises and by the time I left basic training I had built up so much muscle I was pumping out pushups and sit ups and able to run two miles in the expected time. This is what God does with our mind. As we go through each test and get back up we get stronger and stronger in that area. This is called "renewal of your mind." This is how we are transformed, or changed into the form of Christ, by the renewal of our mind daily. Rom 12:2. Every time you fall and get back up, you are renewing your mind. And gradually you will become more and more like Christ.

Mind renewal may not be easy, but God promised to hold us through it. He said he would never leave us nor forsake us (Hebrews 13:5). And he said he would always be with us, even until the ends of the world (Matthew 28:20). The LORD himself can be our strength. Moses said God was his strength and song and has become his salvation (Exodus 15:2). And we know the LORD doesn't even need strength. He is strength. He is the "Self-Existent One." Which means he is God all by himself and exists because of himself.

Revelation 3:8 says, this is the God that opens doors we can't open for ourselves. God will do the things for us that we cannot do for ourselves. But the second part of the verse gives us the key, if we obey his word and do not deny his name. God's name is his character and reputation, therefore, when we need doors opened and to be strengthened supernaturally, we must trust God's reputation and lean into him and we will see wonders. Then we must wait on him. While we are waiting, it can be tempting to turn to another source or to doubt his character, but he said if we wait on him, our strength will be renewed, and we will mount up on wings.

"Here's what I've learned through it all: Don't give up; don't be impatient; be entwined as one with the Lord. Be brave and courageous, and never lose hope. Yes, keep on waiting— for he will never disappoint you!" (Psalms 27:14, TPT). *The Passion Translation* rendering of this verse gives me insight into Isaiah 40:31. "But they that wait upon the LORD shall renew their strength." I looked up the word *wait* in that Scripture and it means *to bind together perhaps by twisting*. I had a difficult time understanding why they would define the word "wait" in that way, and that it would be used in this context. But if in our waiting we become entwined as one with the LORD, not just any lord, the God who exists because of himself and has no god beside him LORD, we will have all the promises that follow. Renewed strength, mounting up on strong wings, flying above our problems and enemies. Running and not becoming weary. Walking without fainting. How could we not if we become one with such power? His power becomes our power and we do exploits. How do you become entwined with God? By turning to him. To become entwined in something you must turn or twist. So when you're twisting in pain turn to God and become entwined with him so that your strength is renewed.

Chapter Sixteen

When the Pain Won't Let Up

"I am the one who has seen the afflictions that come from the rod of the LORD's anger. He has led me into darkness, shutting out all light. He has turned his hand against me again and again, all day long."
Lamentations 3:1-3, NLT

I can so identify with the writer of this lament. My life seems to have been one painful struggle after another. Sometimes I have looked at my life and asked, "can I get a break here?" To no one in particular. Mostly aimed kind of at the heavens. But since it usually seemed to no avail I just kind of let it rise to whomever might choose to listen that day. It was like he has been angry with me all my life and I just can't seem to get on his good side. Ever felt like that? You are who I write this book for. The person that, though you believe in God, it seems as if he doesn't believe in you. Or maybe that's the problem. He believes in us so much, that like with Job, he chose to sick the devil on us. But I often wonder where is my "after this." We read Job's story and see in retrospect that he had an "after this." A period of time that was like what Joel prophesied. Restoration, not just of the stuff he lost, but the years. Only God can restore time. We can sit around and cry because life is painful and full of woe, or we can turn to our amazing powerful God in worship because we know his character.

> Yet I still dare to hope when I remember this: The faithful love of the LORD never ends! His mercies never cease. Great is his faithfulness; his mercies be-

gin afresh each morning. I say to myself, "The LORD is my inheritance; therefore, I will hope in him! The LORD is good to those who depend on him, to those who search for him."

Lamentations 3:21-25, NLT

We can wait in hope when we remember God's character. Then we have to talk to ourselves to cancel the negative thoughts and depression that comes along with suffering. We can "Let God arise." *"Let God arise, let his enemies be scattered…" (Psalms 68:1).* We have to LET God arise. Did you know that you could hinder God? The great I Am who exists because of himself, God all by himself. Little old me (us), we can hinder him. It's not that we are so great, but that God wants us to be participants in the victory because of our relationship with him. It's all about relationship with him. He wants to be our God and he wants us to just be his people. A people for his name, for his reputation among the nations. We and God and God and us. Together. Forever. God is everlasting and he has an everlasting love that he wants to lavish on someone forever. That someone is us if we choose him. If we turn to him and continue to turn to him. In spite of adversity. Turn to him. In spite of our pain. Turn to him. I'm spite of calamity. Turn to him. In spite of our fears. Turn to him. In spite of tribulation. Turn to him. In spite of necessities. Turn to him. In spite of stress. Turn to him. In spite of persecution. Turn to him. In spite of any danger. Turn to him. In every situation God wants us to turn to him and not away, because that is relationship.

We can encourage ourselves when we remember who God is. *"I reflect at night on who you are, O LORD" (Psalms 119:55, NLT).* And when we recall his promises. *"I stay awake through the night, thinking about your promise" (Psalms 119:148, NLT).* And when we think about all the good things he has done: *"I will meditate on your wonderful deeds" (Psalms 119:27, NLT).* And then count our blessings. When the devil tempts you to think about what you don't have, think about all the good that you do have instead. Count your blessings. Name them one by one. It's up to us to change the way we think, *"Let the wicked leave their way of life and change their way of thinking" (Isaiah*

55:7a, GNT). David demonstrated this in 1 Samuel when he came back from war with the Philistines only to find out the Amalekites had taken all the women and children captive, even his. David had knowledge of how cruel and wicked the Amalekites were and what they did to their captives. David's men also knew and were ready to stone David.

"And David was greatly distressed; for the people spake of stoning him, because the soul of all the people was grieved, every man for his sons and for his daughters: but David encouraged himself in the LORD his God" (1 Samuel 30:6). David found himself alone in this trouble because his men were angry with him over losing their families even though David's family was taken captive too. The Message version says, *"And suddenly David was in even worse trouble…(But)David strengthened himself with trust in his God" (1 Samuel 30:4-6, MSG)*

And then he consulted God. David wept with his men, but he didn't stay in his feelings because he knew God's character. It's okay to feel your feelings and mourn your losses, but never forget the character and the power of the God you serve. Sometimes we have to remind ourselves when no one else is around. When we are crying into our pillow at night or run into the bathroom at work. Remember, that God is omnipotent and is willing to use his power to save his people. Remember that you are "his people." Remember that he is with you. Remember that he will not let you be utterly cast down. Remember that he never fails and that not one word from him will ever fall to the ground. And then consult him. Ask him for wisdom and direction for this problem, this situation and believe he will help. For I have never seen the righteous forsaken. *"I have been young, and now am old; Yet have I not seen the righteous forsaken, nor his seed begging bread" (Psalm 37:25).*

Chapter Seventeen

God Prepares Us to Suffer

"But because I have said these things unto you, sorrow hath filled your heart. Nevertheless I tell you the truth; It is expedient for you that I go away: for if I go not away, the Comforter will not come unto you; but if I depart, I will send him unto you."
John 16:6-7

God will prepare us to suffer. Here Jesus was preparing his disciples for the time of his death and the terrible suffering they were going to witness him go through. Not only to witness, but also to understand their suffering. All throughout his ministry Jesus was preparing his disciples for his eventual death and suffering, yet they could not hear. No one really wants to hear that their loved one is going to suffer. And no one really wants to suffer. Jesus didn't want to suffer. In Matthew 26:39, Jesus asked "if there is any way possible that this cup of suffering could pass, please God…" (my paraphrase). But God stuck to the plan. Because there was no other way. The lamb was slain from the foundation of the earth (Rev. 13:8; 1 Peter 18:20) and Jesus came to earth to be that lamb. One of his disciples even got angry with him about it and Jesus had to rebuke him (Matt. 16:22). Can you imagine being angry with Jesus about suffering?

> Verily, verily, I say unto you, That ye shall weep and lament, but the world shall rejoice: and ye shall be sorrowful, but your sorrow shall be turned into joy. These

> things I have spoken unto you, that in me ye might have peace. In the world ye shall have tribulation: but be of good cheer; I have overcome the world.
>
> John 16:20, 33

Many people believe God is not good because of suffering. Either they are suffering or someone they love is and it makes them feel angry at God about it, or just disappointed in him. But it has been my experience, that when we are about to go through a terrible time of suffering God often provides a warning before it begins. It is actually God's goodness that he prepares us to suffer. God wants us to have peace in our suffering, in spite of suffering. So, he gives us warnings through prophesy, dreams, his Word, a sermon, a word of knowledge, to let us know that the thing we are suffering is of him. Sometimes suffering is his will, but our peace in suffering is also his will. Jesus knew his disciples would be confused about the suffering he was about to go through and that they were to witness. He knew how they had totally misconstrued the concept of his kingdom and that they were expecting him to conquer his enemies immediately and overthrow the Roman oppression now.

It can be very confusing to us when we expect God to do one thing and he does something totally different. When we expect God to heal our loved one, but they die instead. When we expect him to make a financial miracle, but we lose the house or go into bankruptcy. When we expect him to change our spouse, but we end up in a messy divorce. What is God doing? Is God who he says he is? Does he love me? Has he ever loved me? Is his word still true? Was it ever true or did I just make this up? Have you ever asked these questions? Maybe not out loud, but in your heart? God knew you would be confused. He often sends warnings that we just don't understand at the time, or sometimes we just miss them. It may be that the day he sent the message that would encourage us through our time of trial was the day our son had a baseball game. We meant to catch the sermon on the rebroadcast, but just never got around to it. Maybe we went to the bathroom, or a baby began to cry, and we got distracted. Maybe we just didn't want to believe it. Like the disciples after Jesus had risen. Two disciples traveled to Emmaus and Jesus walking and talking with them said: *Wasn't it clearly predicted that the Messiah would have to suffer all these things before entering his glory?" (Luke 24:26, NLT).* They totally missed it and Jesus himself had to expound upon all the prophesies about his suffering, death, burial, and resurrection to them as they walked along. Even when we do not get it, he is so merciful to give us another chance.

Elijah didn't get it either. He was despondent and depressed at the threat of Jezebel after God had given him a great victory. Yet God sent an angel to him to prepare him for the great journey he would have to take to Mount Horeb. A journey that would take him over a month. The Bible says 40 days.

> The angel of the Lord came again the second time, and touched him, and said, Arise and eat; because the journey is too great for thee. And he arose, and did eat and drink, and went in the strength of that meat forty days and forty nights unto Horeb the mount of God.
> 1 Kings 19:7-8

Oh, what care God takes with us before we suffer long. He prepares us for the journey with his loving kindness and grace. He is truly Emmanuel.

Chapter Eighteen

When...

The Bible is full of prophesies about suffering, yet I am amazed at the way Christians deal with suffering, myself included. "When" is a sure word. It means something is sure to happen. We can never get it confused with "if". "If" is a big word but "when" is a sure word. The bible is full of "when", and many of them foretell of suffering. Micah said, *"when I sit in darkness" (7:8)*. Isaiah said, *"When the enemy shall come in like a flood" (59:19)*. The writer of 1 Kings said, *"When thy people Israel be smitten down before the enemy... When heaven is shut up, and there is no rain...when thou afflictest them..." (1 Kings 8:33,35)*. James said, *"When your faith is tested..." (James 1:3 NLT)*. Job said, *"When I looked for good, then evil came unto me: And when I looked for light, there came darkness" (Job 30:26)*. The writer of Proverbs wrote, *"When your fear cometh as desolation, and your destruction cometh as a whirlwind; when distress and anguish cometh upon you" (Proverbs 1:27)*. There is a plethora of "when" scriptures that inform, warn, and prepare us for impending pain, yet we manage to disregard them. Just as Jesus' disciples disregarded his many warnings and the scripture's many warnings of Jesus' suffering.

Yet, when all these troubles and tribulations come upon us, there are other "whens" to comfort us. God said, through the prophet Isaiah: *"When thou passest through the waters, I will be with thee* (Emmanuel); *and through the rivers, they shall not overflow thee* (Because he is Jehovah Shammah, he is there): *when thou walkest through the fire, thou shalt not be burned; neither shall the flame kindle upon thee"* (Isaiah

43:2). I absolutely love the way the *New Living Translation* expounds upon this verse: "*When you go through deep waters, I will be with you. When you go through rivers of difficulty, you will not drown. When you walk through the fire of oppression, you will not be burned up; the flames will not consume you.*" But the most comforting word in that scripture is "when." It tells me I do not have to doubt that he will be there. I don't have to fear the deep waters (which is a particular fear of mine), nor do I have to be afraid of difficulties. Some things in life are just hard. But here he says, *I don't have to fear the hard stuff because he will be right there with me.* I don't have to worry about difficult situations because he said when they come, I won't drown in them, or be overwhelmed by them. I have assurance that they will also go away. Kind of like what David said in the 23rd Psalm, "I will fear no evil, even if it's in the valley of the shadow of death." Wow!

"When" gives me peace like nothing else can, because I can be confident in this one sure word that everything is going to be alright. David was that sure when he wrote: "*When the wicked, even mine enemies and my foes, came upon me to eat up my flesh, they stumbled and fell*" *(Psalm 27:2).* They surely came against him to attack him, but he didn't have to worry or be afraid because they didn't have access. When the afflicted cried, the Lord heard him (Psalm 22:24). "*When God bringeth back the captivity of his people, Jacob shall rejoice, and Israel shall be glad*" *(Psalm 53:6).* "*When I cry unto thee* (God), *then shall mine enemies turn back: this I know; for God is for me*" *(Psalm 56:9).* "*But when the fulness of the time was come, God sent forth his Son, made of a woman, made under the law, To redeem them that were under the law, that we might receive the adoption of sons*" *(Galatians 4:4-5).* Yes, "when" is a comforting, sure word. Because when we turn to God when we suffer, he will surely deliver.

Chapter Nineteen

Abundant Life

"The thief cometh not, but for to steal, and to kill, and to destroy: I am come that they might have life, and that they might have it more abundantly"
John 10:10

The *New Living Translation* translates *more abundantly* to *rich and satisfying*. There is nothing richer and more satisfying in life than walking intimately with Jesus. Everything else pales in comparison. Sometimes during great suffering, we are tempted to wonder where is this abundant life you promised me God? We feel as if we have been cheated out of the abundant life God promised to his people. Because what we are walking through doesn't look like the abundance he promised us. But, if we will take the time to quiet our mind and look back over our life and remember all that he brought us through; the bad things that could have happened but didn't, and the good things that did happen but shouldn't have, and yet we are still here, abiding in his kingdom. We will find that the abundance is found in him. He satisfies. In his presence is joy. *"(I)n thy presence is fulness of joy; at thy right hand there are pleasures for evermore"* (Psalms 16:11, emphasis mine).

These feelings of being cheated by life are normal human feelings. This is how the older brother of the "prodigal son" felt when his brother returned and the father threw a party. He couldn't see beyond what he didn't get, to what he had all along. Suffering can do that. It can make the heart so sick that we can't see beyond our current hard situation to see the glorious hand of God over our life all along the way. Nor can we look to the future to understand the glorious results that our suffering will bring about for us and for those who will be impacted by our suffering. *"The wicked watcheth the righteous, and seeketh to slay him" (Psalm 37:32).* The wicked one only wants to kill righteousness in the earth. So, he watches and waits for opportunities to get at the righteous when they are weak.

Therefore, it is imperative to turn to God and worship him in the dark times. He knows the truth about what we are going through. He is the Truth. Jesus is the truth, and God is the truth. *In the beginning was the Word and the Word was with God and the Word was God (John 1:1).* Therefore, the word of God is the truth. *"And ye shall know the truth, and the truth shall make you free" (John 8:32).* The word of God will make us free.

Knowing Jesus through the word is what makes us free. In the text the word "make" and "free" are the same word. Even though the New Testament was written in Greek the writers were Hebrew and when they repeated a word in Hebrew it was meant to emphasize that word. So not only are we *free* we are *truly free*. Also, all the disciples knew that Jesus had said he was the way the truth and the life. But when Jesus said it he said: "I Am" the way the truth and the life… (John 14:6). All Hebrews knew who the "I Am" was. Jesus was stating his oneness with God and the Word all in the same statement.

Contrary to what we feel while suffering, is the knowledge that suffering, when we turn to God in it, will lead us to hope. And how it leads us from disappointment to the satisfaction of the love of God placed in us through the Holy Ghost (Romans 5:3-5). That "rich and satisfied" life he promised. The best thing to do when you are disappointed with the life you are experiencing, the life that doesn't look like the one the preacher was preaching about. When life doesn't look abundant, or "rich and satisfying," is to turn to God and tell him all about it. Pour out your complaint to him in prayer, song, poetry, or prose and wait.

Turning to God in suffering and telling him all about it is more than okay. Actually, there is a name for it. It's called *lamenting*. David lamented in many of the Psalms. The writer of Lamentations lamented. As a matter of fact, if you will read the minor prophets, they were lamenting. To lament is a passionate expression of grief or sorrow. It's very okay to be sorrowful. The problem lies in what we do with our sorrows.

Lamenting is basically singing the "Christian blues." "My baby done left me. And all hope is gone. But Lord I'm gonna praise you so I'm singing this song, I got those biblical blues." Lamenting is complaining about God to God. It's bringing your misery to God with a giant "but" thrown in. "Lord I'm in trouble. I hate this and I don't see no way out. But Lord I know you're good, and you never fail. So, I'm going to sit here and hurt and trust until you bring me out!"

Misery *is* optional. You don't have to stay in misery. I know sometimes life can get so tough that you think you don't have any choice but actually you do. It's just that sometimes you don't like any of your choices. Sometimes you must choose between misery, sadness, discontentment, or some other negative emotion. But you still have choices. Choose the one you can live with and still have joy and peace. Joy and peace do not depend upon your situation changing. If you live in the kingdom of God, you have joy and peace at your disposal. *"For the kingdom of God is not meat and drink; but righteousness, and peace, and joy in the Holy Ghost" (Romans 14:17).* If you're thinking, "no, this is too hard, someone did me wrong and I don't have to take that!" Read Genesis 16, the story of Sarah and Hagar. You could argue that Sarah started it. Or you could argue that Hagar started it. But God told Hagar to adjust her attitude and submit to Sarah. The fact is we are in control of our attitude. We can fix it or change it at our will. We do not have to live in misery. Is there anything too hard for God? Take your attitude, your misery, your problems that are too hard for you to the one that created you, who created everything that is. Lay it down at his feet. Daily, hourly if it takes that. Until your attitude about your circumstances has changed and you are able to live, move, and have your being in him. This is the safest place to be. This is abundance.

I went through a season of this. Someone did me so wrong and I was so angry that I felt I could not be a Christian in that situation. So did king David:

> When my heart was embittered And I was pierced within, Then I was senseless and ignorant; I was like a beast before You. Nevertheless I am continually with You; You have taken hold of my right hand. With Your counsel You will guide me, And afterward receive me to glory. My flesh and my heart may fail, But God is the strength of my heart and my portion forever. But as for me, the nearness of God is my good; I have made the Lord GOD my refuge, That I may tell of all Your works. Psalm 73:21-24, 26, 28, NASB

It wasn't the fact that I didn't know how to forgive. For years people had done me wrong and I had forgiven them. I forgave the person that molested me when I was twelve. I forgave my father for beating me and falsely accusing me when I was eight, which made me afraid to tell anyone that I was being molested at twelve. I forgave the person who raped me when I was an adult. I forgave my ex-husband and his sister for taking my children away from me for eleven years. I forgave the person who molested my daughter and whom I believe molested my sons. I forgave all the women who had slept with my first husband. And many other major and minor infractions that I had faced in my life. I forgave. I let it go. I was able to speak kindly to these people, have Christmas dinner with my ex-husband and laugh and joke with him. I forgave all the years of abuse and never brought it up again. But then, this one evil woman came against me and I became astonished. Not astonished in a good way. Appalled. Stunned. Devastated.

I could not get past the evil she was perpetrating on me. I couldn't forgive or let it go and it made me feel so dirty inside. Because unforgiveness will drag you down into the pit and the mire with it. It muddies your soul. All you can see is darkness and pain, and the pain is unrelenting. And yet I could not let it go. It had its jagged teeth deep in my heart and would not let go. I was wrestling with the powers of darkness personified. Every time she called, and I saw her number come up on my phone, the bile of hatred would rise up in my throat and I could barely bring myself to answer. Yet, I was forced to because this person was my boss. I asked my sister and a couple other prayer warriors to pray for me because the Bible says you should "confess your faults to each other and pray for each other." My sister told me to "just quit the job, it's not worth your soul." But God had already told me to stay. So, I informed her by text. I said, "I'm in between a rock and a hard place." And she texted back: "Well, STAND ON THE ROCK!" I was so caught up in my negative emotions I didn't catch what she was saying as encouragement to stand on the Rock.

I read it in a judgmental tone and went to God with my complaint. I said, "you told us to confess our faults to each other and now *they're* judging me!" Enter another wave of tears and sadness. The truth of what she said didn't hit me until the next morning. It dawned on me that she meant Jesus, my Rock. The Rock of ages. The mountain made of rock that I could hide behind. The chief cornerstone that the builders had set at naught. That Rock. So, I did. I read every scripture they sent me, not just that scripture, I looked up the whole chapter and read it in context. I watched every preaching video they sent me to encourage me, and I sought out my own. I prayed and I cried, and I prayed, and I cried some more. It was a holiday weekend and I spent most of it praying, crying, and watching ministry videos. I turned to the only one who could help me. I didn't let my anger and bitterness turn my heart away from him. He was still good and still God. I worshipped. It is worship to bring your complaint to God. Because it says: I trust you. You *are* good. You *are* sovereign. All power is in your hands. Even if all you can do is cry, cry to him. Hide your soul in him. Let not your heart be troubled. This is what it means to have abundant life. To live a life that is hidden in Christ and nothing can move you.

THE FAMILIAR VALLEY

By: Cynthia Gibson-Dyse

I've been in this valley before,
I've travelled this lonely road.
I've lifted this heavy burden,
I've carried this heavy load.
I've been in this valley before
And seen these woeful sights.
I've smiled through pain filled days,
And cried through tear filled nights.
I've been in this valley before,
Where the rivers of tears run deep.
Where the pain seems never to end,
And the heart continues to weep.
I've stood at the foot of this mountain
And looked at the clouds in the sky.
I've asked these same old questions
Why me Lord? Why me? Why?
I've heard the voice from the mountain
Bid me tenderly... "Come."
Then I heeded the voice from the mountain
Til at last in His arms I was home.

Chapter Twenty

The God of The Valley

"I will return her vineyards to her and transform the Valley of Trouble into a gateway of hope"
Hosea 2:15a, NLT

A valley is a low place, usually found at the foot of a mountain or a range of hills. A valley can also be a low place in your life. A place where the sun doesn't shine as brightly as it does on other people's lives, or as it did on you before you went into the valley. God implored his wayward bride Israel to turn to him by the example of Hosea and his errant spouse. She was in trouble and suffering due to her own rebellion, but God said that if she would just turn to him, he would turn her valley of trouble into a gateway of hope. A gateway gives you access. Access to hope. Hope of an expected end? An ending she could only hope for but could not achieve on her own? I've had some valleys in my life that I faced over and over again, and there were so many times in those valleys I felt hopeless, but when I learned that God was the God of the valley, I was able to live in hope. This is the "gateway of hope," turning to God in your despair. I learned that God greatly loved me, and I began to turn to him in troubled times with trust, and I leaned into him, and he became my rock. *"He is the Rock; his deeds are perfect. Everything he does is just and fair. He is a faithful God who does no wrong; how just and upright he is"! (Deuteronomy 32:4, NLT).* As I walked through the valley and asked my questions, I obtained new perspective. From the position of the valley, I learned that God is sovereign and that everything he does is right. As I cried my tears during those lonely nights, I learned that he is a comforter. As I sat in the loneliness, I learned that he is "a friend that sticketh closer than a brother." As I carried my heavy burdens, I learned that he's a burden bearer. I learned that suffering is inevitable, but misery is optional. You have to suffer to get into this world, suffer while you're here and sometimes suffer to get out. But you do not have to be miserable. Misery is a terrible place to live. In the kingdom of God pain is inevitable but glory is optional. You get to choose whether or not your pain brings forth the glory God intended it to. *"Behold, they shall surely gather together, but not by me: whosoever shall gather together against thee shall fall for thy sake Isaiah"* *(Isa. 54:15).* He said it would surely come (pain, suffering, misery at the hands of others) but he also promised to be there and to work on your behalf.

God is the God that brings water out of the rock. A rock *is* a hard place. But God can bring soft flowing clean water from it. Water is life. *Which turned the rock into a standing water, the flint into a fountain of waters (Psalm 114:8).* We serve the true and living God who can reverse the course of nature making hard things soft and soft things hard. Bringing life out of hard things. And straightening up the things that threaten to swallow us up, things that were meant to drown us.

Chapter Twenty One

The Compassionate Savior

"Then I came to them of the captivity at Tel–abib, that dwelt by the river of Chebar, and I sat where they sat, and remained there astonished among them seven days."
Ezekiel 3:15

The word "Tel-abib" is actually a contraction of two words. One definition of the word "tel" is: *ruins that aren't completely destroyed*. I thank God that even though some things came against me and tried to ruin me, I was not completely destroyed. Things may come against us with the purpose of ruining us, but David said: *"By this I know that thou favourest me, because mine enemy doth not triumph over me" (Psalm 41:11)*. David walked around in confidence, and so can we, because he knew that God was on his side. David had many enemies, but when he looked back over his life, he realized that though he had many enemies, none of them were ever able to ruin him or completely destroy him.

Sometimes when we are in the midst of suffering it may seem as if the situation is going to absolutely annihilate us, but when it's all said and done, and we look back, we are still standing in victory and our enemy is nowhere to be found, because our Compassionate Savior is for us. Jeremiah declared in Lamentations 3:22, *"It is of the Lord's mercies that we are not consumed."* The Hebrew word used for *consumed* in this verse can mean *destroyed*. Jeremiah suffered greatly at the hands of his own people because they did not want to hear about their disobedience and God's judgement. But when he looked back, he understood that the Lord did not allow them to destroy him. This same verse continues to say, *"because his compassions fail not."* It's not just his mercies that hold onto us in suffering, but the Lord is full of compassion. His heart is so full of his creation. We are the "apple of his eye" and when we suffer, he is right there to see us through it.

Another meaning of the word "tel" is *a small mound of anything you can think of.* Also, it can be referred to as an artificial mound formed from the accumulated refuse of generations of people living on the same site for hundreds or thousands of years. It is usually a heap of anything you can think of because each civilization that lived on that spot left traces of their existence. However, they get covered over by each succeeding civilization. As a social worker I have seen many people suffer from the "refuse of many generations" before them leaving their imprint on the psyche. I spend hours counseling people who are suffering from emotional anguish due to generational toxicity and abuse. But Psalm 100:5 says, *"For the Lord is good; his mercy is everlasting; and his truth endureth to all generations."* Other versions say his unending love and faithfulness endures, or lasts to all generations. So, whatever it is, "anything you can think of," God's mercy, and love and faithfulness will cover it.

The Hebrew word *Abib* means *Spring season, or newness of life, or regeneration.* Abib is important in the Hebrew culture. The children of Israel were delivered from slavery in the month Abib, and God commanded them to memorialize it with the Passover. Passover is celebrated in the Spring to this day. Christians also experience Abib. Romans 6:5 states that when we are buried with Christ by baptism we are raised up and should walk in the newness of life.

The two words together (Tel-abib) are an oxymoron. Used in Ezekiel 3:15 it is a picture of Jesus. Jesus experienced "Tel-Abib" as he grew up in this world. He was the "ancient of days" revealed in the book of Daniel, but he came as a new human to make the ruins of mankind new. Abib speaks of newness, fresh starts, and life, and Tel speaks of ancient civilization, and anything you could think of. Just like "I Am." When God told Moses that his name was "I Am," he was saying I Am anything you can think of. If you need direction, I Am a compass. If you need food, I Am bread from heaven. If you need water, I Am water from a rock. Whatever you need me to be, I Am.

Jesus was a newborn baby lying in a manger when he came to earth, but he was also the great "I Am." And he came to earth with the specific purpose of taking our old refuse and making us new. But when he came, he was astonished at the degradation his creation had fallen into, and yet he loved us. He sat where we sat. He felt what we felt. After sitting where we sat, he was able to feel what we feel and have compassion. He was astonished in his humanity at the pain and darkness sin had brought into the world he created.

Astonished! Astonished is when you receive the phone call that your 9-year-old son was just shot and killed by the police. Astonished is when your one-year-old son, whom you nursed at your breasts, is ripped from your grasps, and given to a stranger because you had the audacity to stand up to your abuser. Astonished is when you sit by the bedside of someone you love and watch them leave this earth to enter eternity. Astonished is when you enter your sister's hospital room to see her body changing colors, her eyes glued shut, and the tubes inserted into her leading to important looking machines that are essentially keeping her alive. Astonished is when someone you have loved, nurtured, and cared for over many years turns on you and curses your very name. Astonished is sitting behind bars with scratches and bruises on your body from someone who attacked you, but is now lying in a pool of blood on the coroner's table. Astonished is wiping the blood from between your legs after a brutal assault. Astonished is burying the Egyptian who was fighting with your brother and getting blamed by your very brother for his murder. Astonished is being banished from a kingdom for an act of what you thought was justice, but was considered murder by the powers that be. Have you ever been astonished?

> For we have not an high priest which cannot be touched with the feeling of our infirmities; but was in all points tempted like as we are, yet without sin.
> Hebrews 4:15

> And it came to pass in those days, when Moses was grown, that he went out unto his brethren, and looked on their burdens: and he spied an Egyptian smiting an Hebrew, one of his brethren. Exodus 2:11

Just as Moses left the splendor and ease of the Egyptian palace and went to his brethren and looked on their burdens, God came down from his throne and wrapped himself in flesh to look upon our burdens. He called that body Jesus. Jesus came into this world and experienced grief and anger and rejection and betrayal, thirst, annoyance and love. God already loved the world enough to come down in the flesh. But this love was different, it was human love for other human beings. His deep astonishment brought about a compassion for his people that would hold him to a rugged cross.

This is why you can have such confidence that God can get you to your destination whether he takes you backwards or forward. Because he is the Compassionate Savior. As a matter of fact, he has a history of moving people backwards to their destination. Moses was already in the palace, but he went to the desert then back to the palace to confront Pharaoh.

Abraham went from Ur to Canaan to Egypt back to Canaan (notice this trip did not take 80 years, yet it took the children of Israel 40 years on a one-way trip from Egypt to Canaan). Then Joseph was sent ahead of the family to Egypt. The whole family moved to Egypt, became enslaved only to be delivered to return to Canaan where God promised they would be. And Jesus left heaven to come to earth, to return to heaven.

God is Alpha and Omega. He's the beginning and the end. The first and the last, and the author and finisher of our faith. If he begins a good work in you, he will finish it. *"Being confident of this very thing, that he which hath begun a good work in you will perform it until the day of Jesus Christ" (Philippians 1:6).* Keep in mind that it says if "he" begins it, not you. And it must be a good work. Many people get discouraged because they feel as if their life is not going the way they expected it to turn out. Some people may be suffering from a mental health diagnosis or physical one that shakes their faith. Maybe a child is sick, or maybe death has taken someone you loved, and you just didn't expect life to be so painful. Maybe you've lost a job, or have never been able to obtain one that meets all of your financial expectations. Maybe you live in a neighborhood that you feel is beneath you or is thought of as unsafe by the general population. And maybe you have prayed and prayed and nothing seems to get better. Maybe, just maybe, the good work he is doing is inside of you. Maybe he is teaching you to cope by turning to him daily and desiring him as your daily sustenance. So even if your life seems to be going backwards, don't worry, do not fret, the Compassionate Savior is with you and will lead you to where he wants you to be.

Chapter Twenty Two

Almost...

But as for me, I almost lost my footing. My feet were slipping, and I was almost gone. Then I went into your sanctuary, O God, and I finally understood the destiny of the wicked. Then I realized that my heart was bitter, and I was all torn up inside. I was so foolish and ignorant- I must have seemed like a senseless animal to you. Yet I still belong to you; you hold my right hand."
Psalm 73:2,17,21-23, NLT

Asaph learned some things about himself and about his God in his "almost" moments. Have you ever had an "almost?" We can thank God for the times we "almost" but didn't. When we almost got hit by a car, a stray bullet, a train. When we almost married the person we read about in the paper later on. We almost cursed or almost hit someone. We almost got a divorce. What did your "almost" teach you about yourself and about God?

I almost died by suicide when I fell into such despair over the loss of my children. They had lived with their paternal aunt for so long, and the circumstances just seemed to get more and more dire. When one is bound by depression, suicidal ideation, and darkness, it is extremely hard to think rationally. Once hopelessness gets a foothold in your psyche, it is almost impossible to arise from the spiral that leads to the pit of death. But, you see, "almost" is not a finite word. Almost means whatever it was, *it didn't happen.*

Have you ever done good and had evil returned to you? Have you ever speculated why everyone else seems to be getting all the breaks?

And just why do wicked people seem to prosper and get away with perpetrating evil on others without any consequences? If these questions resonate with you, I suggest you read this whole psalm. Watching the wicked prosper will cause your foot to slip if you're not careful. But with social media, news media, radio, television, tabloids, it is almost impossible not to see wicked people prospering. Even not-so wicked people, if they are prospering and you are not can really bring up some jealousy and insecurities that you didn't even know you had. What do you do?

First you need to recognize it. It takes a little self-awareness to acknowledge when nasty feelings begin to permeate your being. It can also be a little hard to admit, even to yourself that you are entertaining these feelings. But admit you must. However, you may not even realize it until you enter into the sanctuary of God. Being in the presence of the Holy has the power to change you. It can change your view, give you perspective to enable you to change your thinking.

The sanctuary is the place we worship God. It can be in your living room, bedroom, boardroom, kitchen; anywhere you choose to let your heart meet with the Holy God is your sanctuary. Asaph was changed in the sanctuary, and you will be too. When we see the truth (and Jesus is the truth) next to him our little feelings amount to foolishness and senselessness. Things we thought were so important become so insignificant, and all we want to do is bask in his presence. This is when we realize he was there all the time, he was holding us, and we belong to him.

Chapter Twenty Three

What Does it Look Like to be Blessed?

"And Nathanael said unto him, Can there any good thing come out of Nazareth? Philip saith unto him, Come and see."
John 1:46

Blessed can be right up under your nose, and you not even notice it. We tend to look at blessed as obtaining money and prosperity in this life. But blessed is so much more. Mary was considered *"blessed and highly favored"* yet she resided in Nazareth, a city considered by most as lowly. The people were not respected, the town wasn't on a list of "places to go," and yet Mary was blessed. Mary didn't even consider herself as blessed at first. When the angel came to her, she said: *"For he hath regarded the low estate of his handmaiden: For, behold, from henceforth all generations shall call me blessed" (Luke 1:48)*. Lowly? Low estate? Mary was astonished that "The God," the God of her ancestors, Abraham, Isaac, and Jacob; the revered reverenced Holy God of Israel would even look her way. He saw her. A nobody. She may have been poor, she considered herself of low estate. Just any old (young) woman walking around a town that was disregarded by many, and her God saw her. That's amazing in and of itself! Now an Angel (the one who stands before God) is right in front of her, explaining God's plan to save the world through a son that she is going to give birth to.

You may feel as if God does not see you. That you are insignificant, that your life doesn't even matter. But there is a God in heaven that sits high, and looks low, and cares. The writer of 2 Chronicles wrote: *"The eyes of the LORD search the whole earth in order to strengthen those whose hearts are fully committed to him" (16:9a NLT)*. He found such a person in Mary. He chose her to bear his son and provide a home for him while he resided on this earth. And David said: *"Though the Lord be high, yet hath he respect unto the lowly: but the proud he knoweth afar off" (Psalm 138:6)*. God called David *"A man after mine own heart" (Acts 13:22)*.

Mary said, "With all my heart I glorify the Lord! In the depths of who I am I rejoice in God my savior. He has looked with favor on the low status of his servant. Look! From now on, everyone will consider me highly favored" (Luke 1:46-48, CEB).

Blessed doesn't always manifest immediately. Blessed happens from the inside out. You are blessed way before others call you blessed. When you're blessed, you may be the only one who knows it, who understands it at first. But eventually "blessed" manifests. When Mary got the news from the angel, she hurried to her cousin Elizabeth who had received her own miracle. Elizabeth would understand. Mary was so excited to see her cousin Elizabeth. And Elizabeth was just as excited to see Mary. When you're blessed on the inside only, you need the support of those who will believe with you. Elizabeth told Mary, "You believed what the Angel told you and you're going to be blessed for that. Because you believed you're going to get through everything that happened to you as a result. Now Zacharias didn't believe, and he was struck dumb. But because you believed you'll be able to explain to people when the time comes, and you will say exactly the right words. Don't worry if they don't believe you right away. God is going to perform this good work in you until everything comes out right."

Sometimes when we are suffering we feel like we can't be called blessed. Blessed looks better than this. Right? Blessed looks prosperous. Blessed looks mighty. Blessed looks righteous, holy, and brilliant. Right? The mistake we make in this assumption is that "if I do good then good will come to me." This is a faulty assumption.

Where did we get this assumption from? The prophets were good, God-fearing men who walked in the will of God (except Jonah), and yet they suffered greatly (James 5:10). God did not save us for the comfort of our body. God is more concerned about his body *the Church*. Don't get me wrong, we do sometimes attain benefits from righteous living, but that just isn't always the case.

The first mention of "blessed" in the Bible is about fruitfulness and multiplication. Often in the Bible when something was blessed it became fruitful and multiplied. Abraham, after God pronounced blessings upon him, was fruitful, and multiplied. So were Noah and all his children, the fishes in the seas and the animals on the land in creation. Sometimes it happens immediately, as in the fishes and the loaves, but other times "blessed" takes a long time to manifest. As in Abraham's blessing, and Mary, the mother of Jesus' blessing. As in the grain of mustard seed. In Luke 17:6, Jesus told the disciples that they could pluck up sycamine trees by the root if they had just a mustard seed of faith. The disciples knew what an almost impossible task this was because of the deep root systems those trees were known to have. But what he didn't tell them was how long it would take to accomplish this. He just said they would obey. Well, anyone who has ever raised teenagers (or had a husband) can explain to you that obedience doesn't always happen immediately. When you said, "take out the garbage" and they responded "okay," if you didn't set a time limit how can you get angry with them if their obedience does not manifest immediately?

The same with the mountain moving in Matthew chapter 17 verse 20. Jesus never gave a time limit to the removing from hence and setting it yonder. He simply said it would happen. Our problem is that sometimes we have expectations that were not voiced and then we become angry that things didn't manifest the way we imagined them and in comes the blame. Blessed just doesn't always follow our protocols.

"And it came to pass, as he sat at the table with them, he took bread, and blessed it, and brake, and gave to them" Luke 24:30.

If I were the bread, I would have looked at him and said, "I was good before you broke me. I had my nice brown crust just ready to be eaten but you broke me! You didn't even cut me evenly. It would look better if you had cut me. But no, you broke me and got me out here looking crazy to people." Have you ever felt that way? Thought you had it all together? Living your best life, giving God praise and worship. Being a good citizen. Upholding the law. But if you knew who Jesus was, you would have known he didn't break the bread to hurt it, when he blessed it, it was fruitful and multiplied. *"A bruised reed shall he not break, and the smoking flax shall he not quench: he shall bring forth judgment unto truth" (Isaiah 42:3)*. Not only will he not break the bruised reed nor quench the smoking flax, but he will also heal the bruised reed and rekindle the fire that was burning inside of you. God knows when to break you and how to break you. And God is so gracious and tender in our weakness. For what is weaker than a broken reed or smoking flax, or a tender young virgin?

"And the angel came in unto her, and said, Hail, thou that art highly favoured, the Lord is with thee: blessed art thou among women" (Luke 1:28).

Mary did not look blessed in her time. It looked as if Mary had a child out of wedlock. To those close to Joseph, it looked as if Mary had been unfaithful to him and had a baby out of wedlock. It looked like Mary was unappreciative of the "great catch" her father and the elders had secured for her. It looked like Mary was uncaring about the laws and customs of Israel. And for a while, it looked like Mary was alone in this. Who could believe such a thing? Nazareth was poor and despised and Mary was just a girl of lowly estate.

Jacob was the brother that was blessed. He carried the family blessing. Yet he got tricked into marrying the wrong person. The wife he loved was barren for a long time. His son was abducted, his daughter was raped. His descendants were held captive in slavery for 400 years. They had to fight many battles and wander in the wilderness. What about that looks blessed? While Esau is just prospering financially, and his descendants are living peacefully in their own land.

What does it look like to be blessed?

> And he opened his mouth, and taught them, saying, Blessed are the poor in spirit: for theirs is the kingdom of heaven. Blessed are they that mourn: for they shall be comforted. Blessed are the meek: for they shall inherit the earth. Blessed are they which do hunger and thirst after righteousness: for they shall be filled. Blessed are the merciful: for they shall obtain mercy. Blessed are the pure in heart: for they shall see God. Blessed are the peacemakers: for they shall be called the children of God. Blessed are they which are persecuted for righteousness' sake: for theirs is the kingdom of heaven. Blessed are ye, when men shall revile you, and persecute you, and shall say all manner of evil against you falsely, for my sake. Rejoice, and be exceeding glad: for great is your reward in heaven: for so persecuted they the prophets which were before you. Matthew 5:2-12

Jesus began to teach his followers about what the kingdom of God looked like. This teaching may have been very strange to the people following him because God's kingdom does not look like what they assumed it would. The words that were coming out of his mouth must have made the people very confused, and yet they followed. It can also be very difficult for us, in this era to conceive of the kingdom of God, and the way God moves. When we are suffering, we just want it to make sense. But God's ways are not our ways, and neither are his thoughts like ours (Isaiah 55:8). Paul expressed this to the church at Rome: *"How great are God's riches! How deep are his wisdom and knowledge! Who can explain his decisions? Who can understand his ways" (Romans 11:33 GNT)?* And Job, in his suffering said about God: *"On the left hand, where he doth work, but I cannot behold him: he hideth himself on the right hand, that I cannot see him." (Job 23:9).* Maybe it's because God works on the left hand. It takes faith to be blessed. If you have your faith, you have your future. Faith is forged in the furnace of affliction (Isaiah 48:10). Here Job makes the point that God is credible and incredibly worthy. Maybe that's why the writer said, in his letter to the Hebrews: "*But without faith it is impossible to please him: for he that cometh to God must believe that he is, and that he is a rewarder of them that diligently seek him*" *(Hebrews 11:6).*

It takes faith to stay in the furnace, it takes faith to allow them to throw you to a den of lions. It takes faith to be beaten and left for dead. It takes faith to move on after a divorce, the death of a child, the loss of your home, a job, a business. It takes faith to believe that he will reward you if you diligently seek him. But he will. Being "Blessed" is knowing that you need God daily. The ability to depend on him wholly.

Chapter Twenty Four

Chosen for Greatness

Remember Eve, Mary the Mother of Jesus, Jeremiah, Hosea? What would they tell you about suffering? We don't read a lot about either of them being delivered *from* suffering. But we do know that they were delivered *through* suffering. Meaning they walked out their purpose in God then left this earth to be with him in glory, for eternity. We know that Eve lived a long time after the fall. The Bible says that Adam was 130 years old when they had their son Seth and that after that they lived a long time and had many more children. They were walking in their purpose of being fruitful and multiplying. I think one thing they might tell you is that "sometimes we just have to walk out God's promises."

Isaiah 43 says while we're walking it out he'll be with us, we won't get consumed by it, conquered by it, destroyed by it, and it won't be wasted. Eve had a promise from God. Eve didn't have a Bible, a preacher, an APP, social media, a newspaper.... All she had was one word from God. One promise. Her promise was intimately connected to Mary, the mother of Jesus. Mary had a little more than Eve. She had a promise and the word of God in writing. It is not known how Mary had access to the scriptures as females were not taught to read and neither did they attend school. But somehow Mary knew the word of God intimately. And I can imagine as Mary walked past the women in her town who were whispering behind their hands, she may have quoted this psalm to her baby:

"When they walk through the Valley of Weeping, it will become a place of refreshing springs. The autumn rains will clothe it with blessings" (Psalms 84:6, NLT).

Mary told Elizabeth *"henceforth all generations will call me blessed."* She was prophesying her own future. She knew of many of the struggles she would have in agreeing to have this child. She even knew that she could be stoned to death for being an unwed mother. She knew Joseph could divorce her, and that if her community allowed her to live, that she could face a life of poverty, alienation, loneliness, and rejection. But did she know that before all generations called her blessed, her generation would call her son cursed?

Mary was no stranger to pain, but she was also no stranger to scripture. When you cultivate the ability to abide in the word of God, you can walk through anything. The Hebrew boys knew this as they were being cast into the fire, and if you will grasp this truth and hide it deep in your being you will come forth as pure gold.

What would Jeremiah tell us about suffering? Let us go to the source, he put it in writing. When Jeremiah was suffering, even when he thought it was coming at the hands of his God he did not waiver in faith but said:

> This I recall to my mind, therefore have I hope. It is of the Lord's mercies that we are not consumed, because his compassions fail not. They are new every morning: great is thy faithfulness. The Lord is my portion, saith my soul; therefore will I hope in him. The Lord is good unto them that wait for him, to the soul that seeketh him. It is good that a man should both hope and quietly wait for the salvation of the Lord. It is good for a man that he bear the yoke in his youth. For the Lord will not cast off for ever: But though he cause grief, yet will he have compassion according to the multitude of his mercies. For he doth not afflict willingly nor grieve the children of men. Lamentations 3:21-27,31-33

What did Jeremiah do? He remembered God's goodness. God is so good that he took on human form and died on a cross that we would have access to him. Yet, I marvel at the fact that it is so easy for us to be convinced that he isn't good even while wearing a cross around our necks. Jeremiah remembered God's character, his compassion, his mercy and faithfulness. Not only did Jeremiah remember, he also became one with God. He declared that God was his portion, all he had in life. His everything. When God is your everything, all you need is him. Jeremiah held onto hope.

Hosea might tell us to return to the Lord. *"Come, let us return to the Lord. He has torn us to pieces but he will heal us; he has injured us but he will bind up our wounds" (Hosea 6:1)*. Even though Hosea was called by God to suffer in a terribly unhappy marriage, he did not become bitter and angry with God, he did not get offended, he leaned into the pain and trusted in God's healing power. God used Hosea's testimony to demonstrate his love for his people, and to introduce the idea to them that he was bringing salvation to the Gentiles. Paul quoted Hosea in his letter to the Romans, explaining to them about God's sovereignty and ability to save whosoever. I can imagine Hosea reciting this psalm: *Day and night I have only tears for food, while my enemies continually taunt me, saying, "Where is this God of yours?" (42:3, NLT)*. What did Hosea's family think? What did they say about his decision to choose a prostitute for a wife? I'm quite sure Hosea shed some tears some nights, maybe even during the day too. And he probably had some questions for God, this was no easy task he was asked to do. And maybe his enemies did taunt him. Because when you have questions in suffering, sometimes they are coming from "the enemy." As for you, take your questions to God and just trust. Then let trust lead you to praise. Remember all the good God has allowed in your life. David did just that in the following Psalm. *"Let all that I am praise the LORD; may I never forget the good things he does for me" (103:2, NLT)*. God used Hosea, and Hosea was okay with it. Hosea was sold out to his God. Are you? Can you suffer unjustly as Mary, Jeremiah, Hosea, and our ultimate example Jesus?

For God is pleased when, conscious of his will, you

patiently endure unjust treatment. For God called you to do good, even if it means suffering, just as Christ suffered for you. He is your example, and you must follow in his steps. He did not retaliate when he was insulted, nor threaten revenge when he suffered. He left his case in the hands of God, who always judges fairly. 1 Peter 2:19, 21, 23, NLT

Chapter Twenty Five

When you Suffer from False Accusations

"And they began to accuse him, saying, We found this fellow perverting the nation, and forbidding to give tribute to Caesar, saying that he himself is Christ a King."
Luke 23:2

In the 23rd chapter of Luke, we see Jesus being falsely accused over and over again, by the church people. The people who had the nerve to pray to his father. The people who brought the sacrifices of "sinners" to the Holy of Holies. How painful that must have been for him. They had a lot of nerve. The injustice of the Roman taxes and the abuse of the Roman government were the exact reasons they longed for Messiah to come. What a farce! Have you ever had your character assassinated? Has your integrity ever been questioned? What if that same person that accused you falsely found it so easy to believe in others whose integrity was questionable? What if they protected the sleazy person with the same mouth they accused you out of? How would that make you feel? What would you do? While they flung various false accusations out against Jesus, they sang the praises of the thief and murderer they wanted released. On top of the beatings and questioning and dragging from judgement hall to judgement hall, now this. This great emotional pain.

It is very painful to be falsely accused. Yet we often are guilty of this same sin against God. We accuse him of not being good because we are suffering, or we see suffering. Never stopping to consider God's character. We've discussed God's character already. If you skipped that chapter, I suggest you go back and read it. It's worth considering.

God does no wrong, and never has nor ever will do anything wrong, and yet we shake our fist in his face, or simply turn away from him when we face suffering, and bitterness enters our heart.

As humans, maintaining good character in a world such as ours is not an easy feat. Temptation comes on every hand, it would be so easy just to do wrong. Wrong is easy. Right is hard sometimes, most times. And yet, you held on to your integrity in spite of temptation. And then it happens. Someone decides you are not who you say you are. And they tell others. And they tell you. What do you do?

"While they were nailing Jesus to the cross, he prayed over and over, "Father, forgive them, for they don't know what they're doing." The soldiers, after they crucified him, gambled over his clothing." Luke 23:34, TPT

Most versions say, "Jesus prayed Father forgive them." But *The Passion Translation* says he prayed over and over as they were nailing him to the cross, after they had accused him falsely and beat him all night. Over and over again he prayed for them. He prayed through the pain, emotional and physical. And he prayed again. As many times as they accused him, he had forgiveness for them.

But for us not-so-holy humans, it keeps coming back. The emotional pain of false accusations. It keeps coming back. If the person or people who accused you falsely never apologize, never say, I was wrong about you. I'm sorry I hurt you like that. It keeps coming back. And the best thing to do is to follow Jesus's example and pray over and over again "Father, forgive them, they just don't understand." Then pray for yourself. Ask for strength to show them love. Ask for healing in your emotions in that place. And be still and know that he is God, and he is good, and that you know him in the fellowship of his suffering. And after this, you will know him in the resurrection.

DATE RAPE

By Cynthia Gibson-Dyse

You didn't have to tie my hands
(They were already bound by fear).
You didn't have to cut me
(You cut away every defense with your presence).
You didn't have to beat me
(You already trampled my will with your force).
You took that which was not yours to take.
It was not given in love,
It was not given willingly,
It wasn't even given.
It was taken by fear.
Be not deceived, God is not mocked.
You took what belonged to Him.
He will repay!
You took my body,
But you cannot take my Spirit, my Soul, my Essence.
God has preserved me.
He will heal the place that was
Bound, cut and trampled.
And I will spring forth and flower
In the beauty of His presence.

Chapter Twenty Six

Suffering from Sexual Assault

Then he said to Tamar, "Now bring the food into my bedroom and feed it to me here." So Tamar took his favorite dish to him. But as she was feeding him, he grabbed her and demanded, "Come to bed with me, my darling sister." "No, my brother!" she cried. "Don't be foolish! Don't do this to me! Such wicked things aren't done in Israel. Where could I go in my shame? And you would be called one of the greatest fools in Israel. Please, just speak to the king about it, and he will let you marry me." But Amnon wouldn't listen to her, and since he was stronger than she was, he raped her.
II Samuel 13:10-14, NLT

As a social worker I see many people in therapy who are suffering as a result of sexual assault. As a woman, who has been raped I can identify with them. I can understand the total devastation, disappointment, depression, and trauma and distress this act of violence brings to the lives of survivors. Because that is what we are… Survivors. It took me a while to get to the point of being a survivor, because immediately after I was a victim. I struggled with the fact that this could even happen to a Christian. Wasn't I God's child? The child of the King! I was walking in all the light I knew as a single woman in Christ. I wasn't even dating. I was keeping myself pure because of my love for God. Chips and salsa and a good movie from the video store was my Saturday night date. And yet I was raped. How? Why? It didn't make sense!

I wrote the poem *"Date Rape"* trying to process my pain. It helped, but there were still questions in the back of my mind. How could a good God allow something so evil, so violating to happen to his daughter? Did he even care? Where was he while I was being violated? What about my righteous living? Didn't that count for anything? I found comfort and strength in the word of God. First of all the fact that God said vengeance belongs to him. Well, why would God need to take vengeance if nothing bad was ever going to happen to his people? There would be no need for any vengeance, so it stands to reason that bad things will happen to God's children, but we have his assurance that he will take the right recourse on our behalf. He is on our side.

> If it had not been the Lord who was on our side, when men rose up against us: Then they had swallowed us up quick, when their wrath was kindled against us: Then the waters had overwhelmed us, the stream had gone over our soul: Then the proud waters had gone over our soul. Blessed be the Lord, who hath not given us as a prey to their teeth. Our soul is escaped as a bird out of the snare of the fowlers: the snare is broken, and we are escaped. Our help is in the name of the Lord, who made heaven and earth. Psalm 124:2-8

I found my help in the name of the Lord. The Lord's name is his character. The Lord's name is a strong tower, the righteous can run into it and find safety, wholeness, peace, and strength. He is the great I AM. He will be whatever we need him to be when we need him to be it. God is in control, always has been, always will be.

When the earth was formless and void and covered in darkness, we see God above it all, hovering, with a plan. God did not join the darkness. He was above it. He was aware that it existed but was not intimidated by it. It just was. Sometimes the darkness will exist, but it's okay because we have a God, and he has a plan. God hovered above the darkness. He gave it boundaries until the right time to correct it. God's timing is impeccable. We may not understand it but he knows the exact time to act. We are that earth that God hovers above. He sees the darkness around us. He even knows when it invades our place of being, but he has given it boundaries. The darkness cannot overpower the light. The waters could have overwhelmed us, but because God (who is light) hovered above us and was on our side our soul escaped. My soul escaped the darkness that tried to overtake me after I was raped, thank God I knew where to turn. And thank God he was there hovering, waiting for me to turn to him. The snare of pain, depression, despair, and distress was broken, and my soul is intact. Oh, I walked through some darkness, but God knows how to use darkness. *"He bowed the heavens also, and came down: and darkness was under his feet. He made darkness his secret place; his pavilion round about him were dark waters and thick clouds of the skies" (Psalm 18:9, 11)*. God can use darkness to expedite his arrival, he can hide himself in it so the enemy won't see him coming, he can turn it into a poem, a song, or even a book. God can even turn darkness into a ministry. I completely understand why David said, *"I will fear no evil, for thou art with me."* Evil does not stand a chance in the face of our God who is mighty and powerful.

God can take darkness and turn it into a plan to save a whole nation. Joseph was a victim of human trafficking. But God had a plan. Nothing that happens to us is arbitrary. God is not capricious, and he does see the evil deeds perpetrated upon us. He just doesn't worry because he is God almighty and is able to turn any evil plot into glory. *The LORD replies, "I have seen violence done to the helpless, and I have heard the groans of the poor. Now I will rise up to rescue them, as they have longed for me to do" (Psalm 12:5, NLT)*. Remember Hagar? Hagar called God "The God who sees" (El Roi) (Genesis 16:13). He is the God who sees. He saw Noah praying and gave him grace. He saw Moses and Elijah running in fear and made them mighty. He saw David being the least and made him king. And he sees you, and he has a plan for your situation.

Jesus told Peter and all the disciples in Matthew 16:18, that the gates of hell would not be able to prevail against his church. Are you in his church? Then whatever hell has thought up against you will not prevail. To prevail means to succeed, conquer, overcome, and we read in St. John 1:5 that the darkness was not able to overcome the light. Once I made up in my mind that God is good and he is for me, my mind was settled, and my heart was soothed. I was healed from the trauma this vile act brought to my life. We have to settle in our minds over and over, for as many times as it takes, that God is good, and he is for us. We have to settle that he is all powerful (omnipotent) and full of mercy and grace. We can lean into this grace whenever we need to because his grace is truly sufficient for any trial, any test, any problem or thorn, and he will never, never, never leave us nor forsake us.

Chapter Twenty Seven

Suffering from Mental Illness

"I beseech you therefore, brethren, by the mercies of God, that ye present your bodies a living sacrifice, holy, acceptable unto God, which is your reasonable service. And be not conformed to this world: but be ye transformed by the renewing of your mind, that ye may prove what is that good, and acceptable, and perfect, will of God."
Romans 12:1-2

To all God's children suffering from mental illness, I want to encourage you now. And to all of you who love someone suffering from mental illness, this is for you. As a mental health clinician, I am privileged to work with some of the most misunderstood people that God created. Many people in the church do not believe mental illness is real, or they believe it is caused by demons or the devil. They believe that if people with mental illness would just pray harder, try harder, live better, yield to the Spirit, they would be "normal." I speak to the grief and loss you feel concerning your mental health. I speak to the emotional anguish of having a mental health diagnosis, or mental illness whether diagnosed or undiagnosed. If you just have the feeling that you're not "normal" and it makes you sad, I want to encourage you. This chapter is in no wise intended to suggest that you are at fault for your suffering. Or that you need to work harder at your relationship with God or pray harder to get better. For you, the work of therapy may be hard, and you may become discouraged or even question why you are suffering from mental illness. It's to this question I speak.

First of all, there is no "normal" person on this earth. I dare you to find one. Bring them to me and I will help them find their fault. We are all broken because we live in a broken fallen world since Eve and Adam were cast out of the garden. We all have thistles and thorns afflicting us. Some are more obvious than others, but if you will look closely enough, they are there, in all of us. Some of us have become really good at hiding them from others, but when we go to bed at night, they come out and haunt us as we drift off to sleep. Therefore, we should approach those suffering with mental illness with as much compassion as we can find, for there but by the grace of God go I. It could just as easily be you or I suffering in our minds, and if this is you, I urge you not to despair, because you are not alone.

Our brains are part of a broken body. Our brains are not who we are. Our soul is who we are, and it may have been placed inside of a broken body that causes it to suffer from mental illness, but our soul is not going to stay here. Our soul will one day leave this body to be with the Lord in a new body that is perfect:

> For we know that when this earthly tent we live in is taken down (that is, when we die and leave this earthly body), we will have a house in heaven, an eternal body made for us by God himself and not by human hands. We grow weary in our present bodies, and we long to put on our heavenly bodies like new clothing. For we will put on heavenly bodies; we will not be spirits without bodies. While we live in these earthly bodies, we groan and sigh, but it's not that we want to die and get rid of these bodies that clothe us. Rather, we want to put on our new bodies so that these dying bodies will be swallowed up by life.   2 Corinthians 5:1-4, NLT

So, until the day we put on our new body, we may suffer, but we are not alone in it. For God has promised to comfort us, and walk with us, and keep us through suffering. Sometimes we just have to "roll with the punches."

"Rolling with the punches" is an American idiom which is actually instructions on how to take a punch. If the punch is inevitable, instead of standing there braced to take it, if you will allow your body to roll with it, as in, letting your body move in the direction of the punch, it will hurt a lot less. Another term for this is "leaning into the pain." Instead of running from it, we allow it to be, and we flow with it as it washes over us until it is no more. In essence we can do this mentally. Let's say our mind is racing and we just can't sleep, no matter how much we try. Rolling with it means we use the time productively, praying, reading our Bible, memorizing scriptures, listening to podcasts or YouTube messages that encourage us. If you are able to meditate, I would use the time in meditation, however realistically, when the mind is restless gathering it enough to meditate is more frustrating than helpful. It's kind of like asking a runner to run on a broken leg.

The best way to roll with the punch is to just not fight against it. It is what it is. Acknowledge it for what it is and then praise God "for" it. You heard right, for it. "Lord this is painful right now, I hate it, but I love you because you are my God." "Lord, you never fail and your word is truth." "Lord, your rod and your staff they comfort me, even though my life is painful right now, in this moment, I still trust you." "I will lift up my eyes to you because I know my help comes from you only." And to really be bold, take what the enemy says against you and praise God for it. "Lord, my mind is telling me this is too painful and I can't bear it, but you said you are a very present help in trouble."

Jesus our example leaned into the suffering of the cross for us. We witness this in Matthew as he prays in the garden. *He went on a little farther and bowed with his face to the ground, praying, "My Father! If it is possible, let this cup of suffering be taken away from me. Yet I want your will to be done, not mine" (Matthew 26:39, NLT).* Jesus did not want to die nor be separated from God by becoming sin. He asked God for another way, if it was possible. His answer? Silence. There was no other way to redeem mankind and Jesus had to become the sacrificial lamb to purchase our salvation through suffering, sacrifice, and blood. It was the only way. Jesus asked three times, yet each time was met with silence. He asked until his sweat became as drops of blood. He did not want to suffer this way. He knew what awaited him at the cross and it was excruciatingly difficult to get his body to submit. But submit is what he finally did. He did it by focusing on the joy of the result.

"We do this by keeping our eyes on Jesus, the champion who initiates and perfects our faith. Because of the joy awaiting him, he endured the cross, disregarding its shame. Now he is seated in the place of honor beside God's throne" (Hebrews 12:2, NLT).

Suffering is painful. No one chooses to suffer except Jesus. As we see even he requested another choice besides the cup of suffering. But for God, there was no other way but through the path of suffering. So Jesus, being God in the flesh could have decided not to suffer, but instead he chose it. Then he fixed his mind to accept the cup of suffering. We may not choose our road of suffering, but we can accept it. We can fix our mind and set it on higher things to renew it until we are able to bear our lot in life.

If it is any consolation there are many others who would gladly trade places with you, for they are suffering in these broken bodies also. Many people are suffering in broken bodies afflicted with Chronic disease, Epilepsy, Diabetes, high blood pressure, amputations, AIDS, HIV, Lupus, Cancer, PTSD, poverty, religious persecution, abuse, addiction, inordinate sexual attractions and would love to be free but just can't seem to find the way out. The Bible says that *"Many are the afflictions of the righteous: but the Lord delivereth him out of them all" (Psalm 34:19).* God is able to deliver by many or by few. It doesn't matter how large or small the affliction God is able. Never forget the bruised reed and the smoking flax. Jesus is adept at fixing the broken or using them as they are. Remember the fish and the loaves? Every time Jesus broke bread, he blessed it and it multiplied in use and value. How much was five loaves of bread worth in that day? After Jesus multiplied it how much was it worth? It was so valuable that people followed Jesus to have it. If you are broken, put yourself in Jesus' hands then calculate your value through his eyes.

We may suffer in many ways, but Paul said none of these things can separate us from the love of God. And we are more than conquerors in them through the one that loves us (Romans 8:37). Paul also told the Corinthian church that we are in faulty vessels that any excellency found in us would show God's glory and not ours (2 Corinthian's 4:7). And he went on to say that *"We are troubled on every side, yet not distressed; we are perplexed, but not in despair; Persecuted, but not forsaken; cast down, but not destroyed..." (2 Corinthians 4:8,9)*. How are faulty vessels more than victorious? Only through God's supernatural power. *"I can do all things through Christ which strengtheneth me" (Philippians 4:13)*. So do not be ashamed if your brain is broken. Go to therapy *and* pray. Use your coping skills learned in therapy and let these words above bring you comfort.

Chapter Twenty Eight

Triumph in Suffering

This life is a battle between the kingdom of darkness and the Kingdom of God, you must choose a side. *And from the days of John the Baptist until now the kingdom of heaven suffereth violence, and the violent take it by force" (Matthew 11:12).* You have to fight for the kingdom of God. It's not easy. Your enemy is not going to let it be easy. But when things get hard you must stand, brace yourself, and fight, with a pressing attitude; having an "I will not give up" spirit. You have to believe and declare that God is good even when the red notices are staring you in the face. When disease is coursing through your body you have to be convinced that God is good, he is a healer, he is able to make you triumphant.

How many times did he say: "oh ye of little faith" to his disciples? And they were walking with him daily. God in the flesh. Face to face with him every day. Eating with him. Sleeping where he slept. Watching him perform miracles. Yet they struggled with belief. He said blessed are they that believe and have not seen. It's the devil that tries to make us believe we are bothering God because we don't get it on the first try. Jesus prayed three times in one hour about the same situation using the same words. The angels cry "holy, holy, holy," continuously. God is not like us. He never gets tired of us needing him.

I get it, I too have struggled with scriptures that talk about the inability of evil to harm us, or God protecting us from evil when I have had to struggle daily, or have felt defeated many times. But I have come to learn that:

(A). God knows the end from the beginning, and many times he starts with the end and works backwards. For example: *"And God called the light Day, and the darkness he called Night. And the evening and the morning were the first day" (Genesis 1:5)*. God started the first day with evening. Not morning and light as we do. But evening and darkness. And when Moses asked to see God's glory, God showed his back parts to him. *And he said, "I beseech thee, shew me thy glory. And it shall come to pass, while my glory passeth by, that I will put thee in a clift of the rock, and will cover thee with my hand while I pass by: And I will take away mine hand, and thou shalt see my back parts: but my face shall not be seen" (Exodus 33:18, 22-23)*. I looked up this word "face" in the Strong's Concordance and it said the word can be defined as "before" or "front." I have experienced this inability to see God's face in my trials often. He let's me see the end, that I'm going to be triumphant, but the beginning and the middle are a mystery. He often requires that I walk through it, not understanding, not knowing what's next. Just knowing the end, his "back parts." Because without faith it is impossible to please God, and this is faith.

(B). We only know in part. Scripture is a maze. Isaiah says it's *"here a little there a little, line upon line precept upon precept" (Isaiah 28:10, 12)*. So, I get a better picture when I look over in Psalms and see all the writings extolling God for protection and victory. But the one verse that encompasses it all and instills the most hope when I feel like I'm losing the fight is Psalms 41:11: *"By this I know that thou favourest me, because mine enemy doth not triumph over me."* God has the ultimate triumph.

If this is so, what can separate you from the love of God? What would make you turn away from him? He's the only one who can give you victory over your enemy. Paul said nothing, but John recorded that many turned away from him just because of something he said. *At this point many of his disciples turned away and deserted him (John 6:66, NLT)*. One week you're praising him and the next you're crucifying him because he didn't do what you wanted him to do. Jesus never said his people wouldn't suffer, but that suffering would not bring evil, or harm us. David wrote about it: *"The Lord is thy keeper:*

the Lord is thy shade upon thy right hand. The sun shall not smite thee by day, nor the moon by night. The Lord shall preserve thee from all evil: he shall preserve thy soul" (Psalms 121:5-7).

We might even look barren and unfruitful. But just because you look barren and unfruitful doesn't mean you are. Second Peter 1:5-8 says, if we diligently "...add to our faith virtue; knowledge; patience; godliness; brotherly kindness; and charity; and if we let these things be in us, and abound, then it would make us to be neither barren nor unfruitful in the knowledge of our Lord Jesus Christ." To diligently add to your faith is to seek him with your whole heart.

"And, behold, thy cousin Elisabeth, she hath also conceived a son in her old age: and this is the sixth month with her, who was called barren" (Luke 1:36).

She was barren but she wasn't. She just hadn't conceived yet. Just because people call you something, it doesn't make you that. Just because the enemy calls you something, you don't have to receive it. God has the final say so. No matter how long he waits to act on your behalf, rest assured that he does know how, and he will in his timing. Your job, your main job (and this is a big one) is to keep the faith. Faith in God. Faith in his promises. *For with God nothing shall be impossible (Luke 1:37).*

In the 29th chapter of the book of Jeremiah, God warned the children of Israel that they were going to be in captivity a long time. Seventy years in fact. Most of them would be dead and their children would be old when their captivity ended. But God told them through the prophet Isaiah that if they sought him with their whole heart, he would be found of them and he would turn away their captivity. However, they chose not to believe his prophets. They wanted to believe the false prophets and dreams that said: "God wants you to be blessed." "God wants you to be happy." They could not believe that God would allow them to suffer like that. But happiness is not God's highest goal, relationship with him is. God knows, no he sets the parameters of our suffering. He has a set time. Sometimes it's a long time. Sometimes it just feels like a long time. Nevertheless, you can always rest assured that he is good, and he is God, and you can trust him. You can invite him in to sit with you in the darkness. Micah knew that. "…*When I sit in darkness the lord will be a light unto me" (Micah 7:8b)*. And because of this, he went on to say: *Then my enemies will see that the Lord is on my side. They will be ashamed that they taunted me, saying, "So where is the Lord — that God of yours?" With my own eyes I will see their downfall; they will be trampled like mud in the streets" (Micah 7:10, NLT)*. Micah knew that holding on to God would cause him to triumph.

Chapter Twenty Nine

The Progression of Trouble

"And it came to pass, when Joseph was come unto his brethren, that they stript Joseph out of his coat, his coat of many colours that was on him."
Genesis 37:23

"And she caught him by his garment, saying, Lie with me: and he left his garment in her hand, and fled, and got him out." Genesis 39:12

"Then Pharaoh sent and called Joseph, and they brought him hastily out of the dungeon: and he shaved himself, and changed his raiment, and came in unto Pharaoh." Genesis 41:14

"And Pharaoh took off his ring from his hand, and put it upon Joseph's hand, and arrayed him in vestures of fine linen, and put a gold chain about his neck." Genesis 41:42

"Then we turned and set out for the wilderness by the way of the Red Sea, just as the LORD had told me; and we circled Mount Seir for many days. And the LORD spoke to me, saying, 'You have circled this mountain long enough; turn northward.'"
Deuteronomy 2:1-3, AMP

Ever feel like you're going through the same trial over and over. Someone was always taking from Joseph. Taking his most personal possession, stripping him. Does your life feel like an endless cycle? You keep doing the same thing over and over? Never making any progress, never getting any better? You keep marrying the same person, having the same money problems, making the same poor choices. You pray, you even fast, but nothing seems to ever get better? You try to do all the right things, yet you continue to get the same results? Job said it like this: *"Man that is born of a woman is of few days, and full of trouble" (Job 14:1)*. The children of Israel must have felt that way as they journeyed round and round the same mountain. If Moses wife was there, I am sure she nagged him to just stop and ask for directions. But we know Moses had an inner compass, a relationship with God. "The" God. The God that sits high and looks low. The same God that saw the disciples in the ship tossing with the waves in the storm.

> And he was in the hinder part of the ship, asleep on a pillow: and they awake him, and say unto him, Master, carest thou not that we perish?   Mark 4:38

> And when he had sent them away, he departed into a mountain to pray. And when even was come, the ship was in the midst of the sea, and he alone on the land. And he saw them toiling in rowing; for the wind was contrary unto them: and about the fourth watch of the night he cometh unto them, walking upon the sea, and would have passed by them.   Mark 6:46-48

When Jesus is man he's sleeping in our ship, but when he's God he's in the mountain watching it. God watches us carefully and knows our every need. Yet when trouble comes we forget who he is. We forget whose we are. We become afraid, frustrated, angry, disappointed, disenchanted, anxious, everything our counterparts (the children of Israel) were in the wilderness. But their leader, Moses was not. He simply followed God. Why is that so hard for us? To follow a God that already knows the end from the beginning. He shows us in his word how trouble progresses, and that the latter end is always better. Look at the story of Joseph, Old Testament Joseph. Joseph with the coat.

Joe began his story wearing a beautiful coat of many colors that was fashioned by his father. His earthly father. He was footloose and fancy free, walking around the family complex in his bright new coat which clearly showed everyone that he was his father's favorite. This made his brothers jealous, so they kidnapped him, stripped him of his coat and sold him into slavery. The next time we see Joseph he has a new coat, but again, someone strips it away from him. I guess coats really enhanced Joseph's beauty and it made his boss's wife lust after him. But Joseph had too much integrity to allow her to entice him so he began to avoid her. But the day came that he could not avoid her and she cornered him in her home and he got away, barely. He had to leave his coat to get away from her grasp. Since she could not get him to come down to her level, she lied on him and he was sent to prison. In prison he had to put on prison garb. Which probably involved some kind of coat. When he is summoned by the king, Joseph willingly takes this coat off and changes himself into a better coat to be presentable before the king. And the next time we see Joseph the king is arraying Joseph in vestures (multiple) of fine linen and jewelry and gold, who needs a coat? Now Joseph has all the coats he wants and plenty to share. He could open a coat store if he wanted to.

How many times have you had a pity party about what you don't have but other people do? Or how many times have you become depressed over what you lost, not knowing that God is your portion? Joseph must have made God his portion during the time that he was down and out. All while people were doing him wrong, falsely accusing him, stripping him, trafficking him. To be able to forgive like Joseph did, someone had to be praying and seeking God. I am a forgiving person, but I would have reached my limit a long time ago. Like while I was in the pit after my brothers sold me. I would have been seething, fantasizing about ways to get them back if I ever saw them again. The Bible doesn't tell us of Joseph's prayer life like it does Daniel's but the Bible does say that if we pray in secret the Lord will reward us openly (Matthew 6:6).

Still don't understand the progression of trouble? What about Mary, the mother of Jesus and her Joseph? When we first encounter Mary, she is just minding her business, being a virgin, preparing for her wedding. Mary was also another secret prayer warrior. What greater reward than to be called the mother of the Messiah. All Jewish women desired this great honor since Eve was promised this in the

Garden. But what they didn't understand was the suffering that it entailed. Neither were they prepared for it. God saw in Mary the person he wanted to raise his son. A person soft enough to be a mother to his child, but strong enough to bear the burden of the immense suffering involved.

In the matter of time it takes to have a conversation with an angel, Mary goes from espoused wife to despised adulteress (supposed). Her future husband did not believe her story. He was ready to divorce her, quietly, because he was a just man. But in the matter of time it takes to have a conversation with an angel in a dream, Joseph goes from well-respected artisan, (he was of the house of David, royal lineage) to Joe the carpenter who conceivably knocked up Mary before the marriage ceremony. Shame, shame, shame! Imagine all the feelings coursing through their bodies. As Mary's body changes physically and emotionally she has to cope with all the gossip, lies, rejection, abandonment and fear for the life of her child, and her own. And Joseph had to cope with fear for Mary, the unborn child, and his own reputation (who will hire me now?). They lived in a small town with plenty of judgmental people who would gladly take it upon themselves to provide proper punishment for sins.

Later God provides a way for them to get out of the hotbed of gossip by sending them to Bethlehem to give birth as prophesied in the holy scriptures. And even though the journey may have been difficult and possibly even treacherous, his grace was sufficient, and they made it in time for Mary to give birth. But where? They are provided with shelter for the event, not ideal, but just enough. And unbeknownst to them the perfect setting for the lamb of God to be born…a stable. After the birth, while still in the stable they encounter a wonderful confirmation that they are still in the will of God. Shepherds arrive at the stable to worship their son. Their little newborn baby boy is being worshipped by people they never met, but were instructed by an angel to go see him. After this the shepherds went on social media telling all their contacts that the savior was born and they were the first to see him, *#now who's a dirty stinking shepherd? #howyalikemenow?*

Now contrary to popular belief, the wise men were not there in the stable. It took them a while to get their cars started and they took the scenic route. Jesus was probably around two years old according to the scriptures and when Herod had all the children murdered. Mary and Joseph and Jesus lived in a house in Bethlehem from Jesus' infancy until around two.

> And when they were come into the house, they saw the young child with Mary his mother, and fell down, and worshipped him: and when they had opened their treasures, they presented unto him gifts; gold, and frankincense, and myrrh. Matthew 2:11

This scripture showed us the progression of trouble. When Joseph and Mary first came to Bethlehem, they had to resort to Mary giving birth in a stable. But in a few years, they had a house and Magi were coming to worship their first-born child bringing gold, and frankincense, and myrrh. Gentile royalty recognized the birth of the savior of the world and came to worship him, bringing him gifts, expensive gifts, that God had provided through them to financially support the raising of his child as they ran for their child's life to Egypt.

The progression of trouble helps us understand that:

> ...we glory in tribulations also: knowing that tribulation worketh patience; And patience, experience; and experience, hope: And hope maketh not ashamed; because the love of God is shed abroad in our hearts by the Holy Ghost which is given unto us. Romans 5:3b-5

There is a trajectory to suffering that brings us to hope. We have nothing to be ashamed of when we have hope. Even if our suffering takes us to the lowest pit and strips everything from us, or makes us look as if we do not have any integrity from false accusations. Hope keeps the spirit alive. Hope helps us put one foot in front of the other. It is the loss of hope that makes people take their own life. But Jeremiah said when he recalls the fact that the Lord's mercies keep us from being consumed by our suffering, his hope springs to life and infuses life into his spirit. So,

> Consider it nothing but joy, my brothers and sisters, whenever you fall into various trials. Be assured that the testing of your faith [through experience] produces endurance [leading to spiritual maturity, and inner peace]. And let endurance have its perfect result and do a thorough work, so that you may be perfect and completely developed [in your faith], lacking in nothing
>
> James 1:2-4, AMP

Chapter Thirty

Low Estate

"For he hath regarded the low estate of his handmaiden: for, behold, from henceforth all generations shall call me blessed."
Luke 1:48

One can only speculate that Mary the mother of Jesus was poor. She says it herself in the above statement, and the type of sacrifice she brought to the temple after the birth of Jesus also indicates that she may have been poor because the Bible also says:

> If a woman cannot afford to bring a lamb, she must bring two turtledoves or two young pigeons.
> Leviticus 12:8a, NLT

> And when the days of her purification according to the law of Moses were accomplished, they brought him to Jerusalem, to present him to the Lord; and to offer a sacrifice according to that which is said in the law of the Lord, A pair of turtledoves, or two young pigeons.
> Luke 2:22, 24

She was unaware that she had given birth to The Lamb. She still felt that she was of low estate. It's evidenced by the surprise she expresses when they arrive at the temple and Simeon prophesied over him.

She probably felt that she was of low estate because she lived in a town that people looked down on the citizens. In Jesus' day Nazareth wasn't the place to be. No tourists vacationed there. You didn't see it on the news. No paparazzi filled the town searching for celebrities. Yet God saw fit to have his son raised there.

The only thing the Bible says about Joseph is that he was a just man, and he was of the lineage of king David. "...and Jacob begat Joseph the husband of Mary, of whom was born Jesus, who is called Christ. So all the generations from Abraham to David are fourteen generations; and from David until the carrying away into Babylon are fourteen generations; and from the carrying away into Babylon unto Christ are fourteen generations" (Matthew 1:16-1).

Joseph was essentially a prince. What was a Prince doing in Nazareth? You can be royalty and find yourself in dire circumstances. Remember Mephibosheth? He found himself in Lodebar. What about king David? How many times do we read about him in dire circumstances? He wrote "many are the afflictions of the righteous."

You can be a queen and find yourself in a low estate:

> "If it please the king, let there go a royal commandment from him, and let it be written among the laws of the Persians and the Medes, that it be not altered, That Vashti come no more before king Ahasuerus; and let the king give her royal estate unto another that is better than she." Esther 1:19

Your royal estate can be snatched from you in a moment by your enemies. This is how Joseph the son of Jacob went from favorite son to a slave in a matter of moments.

You can also be "just" or upright, and still end up in a lowly state. The Bible describes Joseph as a "just" man. What brought them low? Purpose. Purpose can take your royal self and bring it to a low estate. But God had a plan for each of them because when you have purpose, you can't stay there.

"Then Peter said, Silver and gold have I none; but such as I have give I thee: In the name of Jesus Christ of Nazareth rise up and walk." Acts 3:6

Now Nazareth is a good thing. It's the place to be. There's healing in the name of the one who lived there. There are Nazareth bumper stickers. "Jesus lived here." Nazareth T-shirts. Paparazzi skulk in the alleys attempting to snap a picture of anyone related to Jesus. Because in his name lepers are walking and leaping and praising God. God is the one that can lift us from our low estate. Ethan the Ezrahite said: *"Thou hast a mighty arm: strong is thy hand, and high is thy right hand" (Psalms 89:13).* God our own God who is above nature and beings, whose power is unbeatable, and wisdom is unsearchable, and knowledge is unfathomable will raise us up from our low estate.

Chapter Thirty One

Nevertheless

Now Jesus loved Martha, and her sister, and Lazarus. When he had heard therefore that he was sick, he abode two days still in the same place where he was.
John 11:5-6

This must have been very hard for Jesus as a man. As God, he knew that everything was going to be alright. He knows the end from the beginning. He has already set the perfect timing of the outcome and he does not worry. God was the originator of "set it and forget it." Nevertheless, as a human this had to hurt. Not that he didn't believe the outcome God had already revealed to him. You can believe God, have faith, trust, all that, and still have emotional pain in the midst of the problem. You think Jesus didn't know that Mary and Martha were going to be angry with him? Do you think that it didn't hurt him to know that the people he loved most were angry with him? When you are standing on the promises of God sometimes the people you love will get angry with you. They don't see what you see and know what you know, and their faith is not where yours is, and nevertheless you must stand.

Do you think when Noah was building the ark that he didn't have relatives and friends that thought he was crazy? Do you think they didn't beg him to stop acting so foolishly? Job's wife lambasted him about holding on to his faith when his problem looked so dire. Not realizing she was the foolish one. Because if God is who he says he is, then blind eyes can still be opened. Deaf ears will still hear. Hearts will still be fixed. And minds will still be regulated. Nevertheless, while you wait it can be so painful to live in the reality of circumstances that do not look like what God told you. Nevertheless, it is up to us to hold fast to the faith that was delivered unto the saints. The measure of faith God distributed to us at birth, and that hopefully we have grown by hearing his Word.

The word "hear" in Hebrew also means to obey. When we listen to anointed preachers; when we study the word of God and hear his voice speaking to us in the scripture; if we obey his voice our faith will grow as the mustard seed grows, where birds can land in it and make their nest. Birds can't make a nest in a mustard seed, it's too tiny, but when it matures into a mustard tree it's available to provide rest and shelter for the birds, just as our mature faith provides rest and ministry for the weary souls that will come to us for shelter.

Noah heard the word of the Lord and continued to build the ark. Even though he had never seen rain, never heard of it, he stood flatfooted on what he knew. Because he believed that there would be a performance of the things which were told him from the Lord. And nevertheless, he built an ark and saved humanity. Just as Mary did. Mary knew that babies didn't come from virgins, nevertheless she heard a Word from the Lord that said that one would, and he would save his people from their sins. Her espoused husband knew how babies were made, nevertheless once he heard from the Lord he stood by her side and protected her and the child from the onslaught of the enemy.

Joshua knew that you didn't win battles with yelling and marching, nevertheless when he heard a Word from the Lord, he was victorious. How about David killing a giant with only a rock, and a sling? Who do you think whispered to him *"you can do this David; I'll be with you?"* God isn't even mentioned in the book of Esther, nevertheless we see his hand moving, orchestrating the deliverance of his people through providence. Providence is code for "God is in control."

Nevertheless, means *though* but slightly different. It means still. I believe he's still going to do it even though I don't see it right now. I believe God still loves me though I lost two houses, two husbands, two children, a mother, a sister, a father, friends, respect. Nevertheless, also means *whatever*! Whatever devil. Whatever you want to throw at me I will be victorious. As a clinician I hate it when my teenage clients say "whatever" because they are trying to portray to me that they don't care, and I know they really do. However, I can totally relate to this ploy when speaking to the enemy of my soul. Whatever! Nevertheless, means anything, and everything, at the same time. Nevertheless, means that something could have stood in the way of something happening but didn't, and the thing happened anyway. Such as: "my enemy wanted me to fail, nevertheless God stood by my side, and I was victorious through his love for me." I can say like Paul to the Philippian church:

> Yea doubtless, and I count all things but loss for the excellency of the knowledge of Christ Jesus my Lord: for whom I have suffered the loss of all things, and do count them but dung, that I may win Christ, And be found in him, not having mine own righteousness, which is of the law, but that which is through the faith of Christ, the righteousness which is of God by faith: That I may know him, and the power of his resurrection, and the fellowship of his sufferings, being made conformable unto his death.
>
> Philippians 3:8-10

Not only do I believe that he still loves me, but I still love him, with all my heart. He has never failed me, and I know he never will, because it is not even possible for my God to fail. I continue to read his Word daily, and pray, and worship him as my savior. I continuously trust and lean on his everlasting arms whether I am struggling, suffering, or at peace.

> For the which cause I also suffer these things: nevertheless I am not ashamed: for I know whom I have believed, and am persuaded that he is able to keep that which I have committed unto him against that day.
>
> 2 Timothy 1:12

I am crucified with Christ: nevertheless I live; yet not I, but Christ liveth in me: and the life which I now live in the flesh I live by the faith of the Son of God, who loved me, and gave himself for me.

Galatians 2:20

Epilog

Called to Suffer,

Chosen for Greatness

I wrote this book for the believer who is suffering and is struggling with the why. I did not write this book for unbelievers. Unbelievers are going to blame God, or blame the victim, or blame someone. But the believer who is suffering needs some answers. I don't have all the answers, but I have some of the vital ones. I wrote this book as a springboard for believers to get enough answers to turn in the direction of God who is able to give them the answers they need, the way they need to hear it. So that he can finish the good work he began in them.

> And others had trial of cruel mockings and scourgings, yea, moreover of bonds and imprisonment: They were stoned, they were sawn asunder, were tempted, were slain with the sword: they wandered about in sheepskins and goatskins; being destitute, afflicted, tormented; (Of whom the world was not worthy:) they wandered in deserts, and in mountains, and in dens and caves of the earth. And these all, having obtained a good report through faith, received not the promise: God having provided some better thing for us, that they without us should not be made perfect. Hebrews 11:36-40

Just because we suffer does not negate the fact that God is real. Or that he loves us. The Bible records that there were individuals who suffered horrifically, some not receiving relief in this world. Yet, they will reign with us in the kingdom to come. *Blessed is the man that endureth temptation: for when he is tried, he shall receive the crown of life, which the Lord hath promised to them that love him (James 1:12).*

The 23rd Psalm records God's true loving care for his people. David equated his love for us with the shepherd's tender care of the sheep. I love this Psalm and meditate on it often. I wrote some insights from my meditation into David's words:

"The LORD (Self-Existent, Eternal One) is m*y shepherd* (my provider, protector, keeper, caretaker)*; I shall not want."* (I call him Shepherd because he takes good care of me. He takes good care of me because he is a good Shepherd). *"He maketh me to lie down in green pastures: He leadeth me beside the still waters."* (He takes good meticulous, diligent care of me by considering my needs, what is best for me. I may be attracted to the sound of rushing water, but he leads me to still, quiet waters that I can drink from and not be harmed. God is *for* me. Even though I am lowly and unimportant to others, I am important to him. My life matters to him, and he shows it in his care for me. If he leads me beside still waters, it means he's there. How can one lead without being there with you?) *He restoreth my soul* (it is God that brought my soul back from the pits of hell.

When I thought I would lose my mind, he held onto it and restored it to my body and allowed me to live another day to see his goodness) *he leadeth me in the paths of righteousness* (he leads, never pushing, he takes the lead and he goes before me making straight paths for my feet so I won't stumble or fear) *for his name's sake* (it wasn't just about me, it was about his character, his goodness. His name is his character, and it makes me want to take right paths to please him). *Yea, though I walk through the valley of the shadow of death, I will fear no evil:* (I feel fear, natural fear in my body, because I have experienced many unsafe situations. So did David. But David found his safety in God. As God has shown up consistently in my valleys of the shadows of death. I have learned to trust him more and more. I will fear no evil. "Will" speaks to the future. Once I learn to completely trust God and lean not to my own understanding, once I have let perfect love cast out all fear, I will fear no evil) *for thou art with me; thy rod and thy staff they comfort me.* (When I abide in him I know he is with me. When he is with me, I derive comfort from his rod and his staff. His rod corrects me when my feet would wander and cause me to stray away from what I know is right. His rod can be very painful, but his staff supports and sustains me, gently corrals me and keeps me moving in the right direction) *Thou preparest a table before me in the presence of mine enemies:* (I marvel that I sit at the King's table eating from his Word freely when others who were my enemies have gone back and cannot seem to find a place at the table. I pray for them because food that is shared brings more pleasure) *thou anointest my head with oil;* (protection, he knows how to protect his sheep) *my cup runneth over* (my cup of gratitude that I am his and he is mine continues to run over daily. I can never thank him enough for including me in his flock). *Surely goodness and mercy shall follow me all the days of my life: and I will dwell in the house of the Lord forever.*

> Now that we know what we have—Jesus, this great High Priest with ready access to God—let's not let it slip through our fingers. We don't have a priest who is out of touch with our reality. He's been through weakness and testing, experienced it all—all but the sin. So let's walk right up to him and get what he is so ready to give. Take the mercy, accept the help.
> Hebrews 4:14-16, MSG

My prayer: LORD (Self-Existent One, God all by yourself, Master, Great I Am,) I need you to come down and sit with me in this misery. I need you to guide me with thine eye. I need you to hide me in your bosom. I need you, and I ask you to *"Make me glad according to the days wherein you have afflicted me, and the years wherein I have seen evil"* (*Psalm 90:15*) in the name of Jesus. AMEN

About the Publisher

Let *Life to Legacy* bring your story to literary life! We offer the following publishing services: manuscript development, editing, transcription services, ghost-writing, cover design, copyright services, ISBN assignment, worldwide distribution, and eBook conversion.

We make the publishing process easy. Throughout production, we keep the author informed every step of the way. Even if you do not have a manuscript, that's not a problem for us. We can ghost-write your book from audio recordings or legible handwritten documents. Whether print-on-demand or trade publishing, we have packages to meet your publishing needs. At *Life to Legacy*, we take the stress out of becoming a published author.

Unlike other *so-called* publishers, we do more than just print books. Our books and eBooks are distributed to book buyers, distributors, and online retailers throughout the world—this is real publishing! Call us today for a free quote.

Please visit our website
www.Life2Legacy.com

or call us
708-272-4444

Send e-mail inquiries
Life2Legacybooks@att.net

www.ingramcontent.com/pod-product-compliance
Lightning Source LLC
Chambersburg PA
CBHW030138170426

43199CB00008B/122